TREACHEROUS JOURNEY

My Escape From Ethiopia

TREACHEROUS JOURNEY

My Escape From Ethiopia

Shmuel Avraham
with
Arlene Kushner

Shapolsky Publishing, Inc.
56 East 11th Street,
New York, NY 10003
(212) 505-2505

A Shapolsky Book
Published by Shapolsky Books
A division of Steimatzky Publishing of North America, Inc.

For any additional information, contact:
Steimatzky Publishing of North America, Inc.
56 East 11th Street, NY, NY 10003

Typography by Image Tech, Milwaukee, Wisconsin

10 9 8 7 6 5 4 3 2 1

First Edition 1986

Library of Congress Cataloging in Publication Data
Avraham, Shmuel, 1945 -

Shmuel Avraham: My Escape from Ethiopia

1. Avraham, Shmuel with Kushner, Arlene 2. Biography
3. Illustrations 4. Escape from Ethiopia 5. Jewish history of Ethiopia
6. Jewish education in Ethiopia

ISBN: 0-933503-46-5
LOC: 86-60182

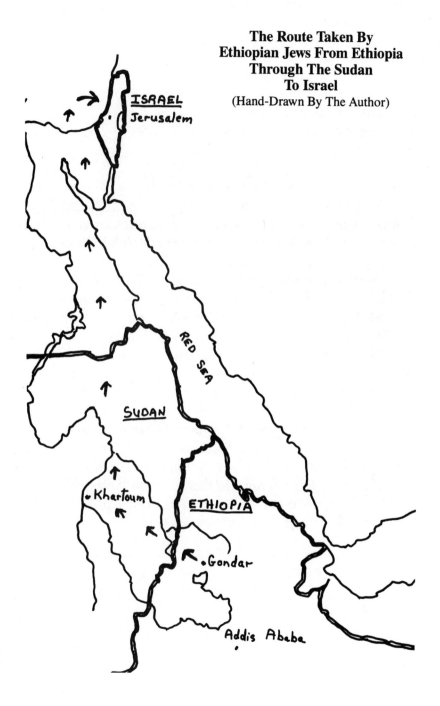

**The Route Taken By
Ethiopian Jews From Ethiopia
Through The Sudan
To Israel**
(Hand-Drawn By The Author)

ISRAEL
Jerusalem

RED SEA

SUDAN

Khartoum

ETHIOPIA

Gondar

Addis Abeba

0 _____ 100 miles

Author's Note

As I write, thousands of Ethiopian Jews, having paid a huge price in suffering and sacrifice, have finally made their way to Israel. Every one of them who left Ethiopia the hard way has his own story to tell.

And their suffering is not yet over. Those who have arrived in Israel still must find the means to participate as full partners in the Jewish State. The thousands still trapped in Ethiopia are awaiting their turn to be free.

What I have written is true. But this is my own story, and because my primary concern is for my people, I have protected them by disguising names wherever it was appropriate.

"To everything there is a season." This, my first book, is not meant to be a complete accounting of the emigration of Ethiopian Jewry, or their absorption by Israel; that process is still unfolding. I am hopeful that work on their behalf will achieve increasingly positive results. And I pray that the season of their suffering will soon be over.

Shmuel Avraham
Israel, 1986

This book is dedicated to all those Ethiopian Jews
who gave their lives on the way home.

Collaborator's Note

... "I hope the new world will be in favor of me and my people ... help me pray for that."

So wrote Shmuel Avraham, in a letter to me, over a year ago. When he invited me to collaborate on a book with him, I was delighted, because he was a man whom I respected and trusted. Our friendship—our capacity for mutual understanding—had developed over a period of months and had required genuine effort on both our parts.

In the months since this project was begun, I have come to realize that Shmuel is the most quintessentially Jewish soul I have ever known. What does being Jewish mean if not to possess strong inner faith, an innate sense of justice, a reverence for human life, a love of learning, and a resolve to give to others? This book belongs to him.

Arlene Kushner
New Jersey, 1986

C O N T E N T S

Chapter 1
THE BEGINNING xi

Chapter 2
LIFE IN MY VILLAGE 13

Chapter 3
BEYOND THE VILLAGE 29

Chapter 4
JEWISH EDUCATION FOR THE PEOPLE 43

Chapter 5
THE DESTRUCTION 53

Chapter 6
ESCAPE 111

Chapter 7
THE OTHER COUNTRY 143

Chapter 8
EPILOGUE: ISRAEL 151

Migration Routes of Jews
From Judah (Ancient Israel)
To Abyssinia (Ethiopia),
586 B.C.E. - 525 C.E.
(Hand-Drawn By The Author)

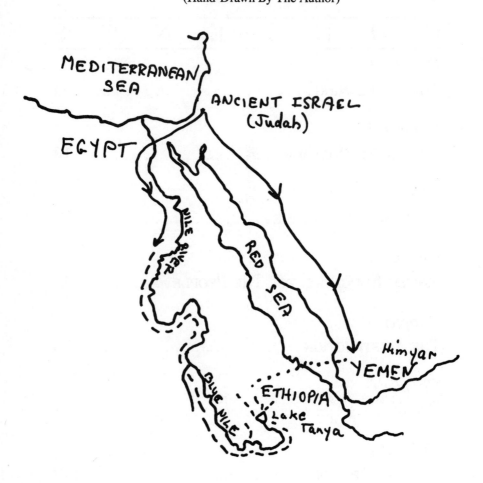

Legend of Migration Routes

——————— 586 B.C.E. — After the destruction of the First Temple

---------------- 300 B.C.E. — After the expulsion of the Persians from Egypt

· · · · · · · · · · 525 C.E.   — During the war between Ethiopia and Yemen

1

The Beginning

Ethiopia, As Situated
Geographically Within Africa
(Hand-Drawn By The Author)

Major Jewish Population Centers
In Ethiopia
(Hand-Drawn By The Author)

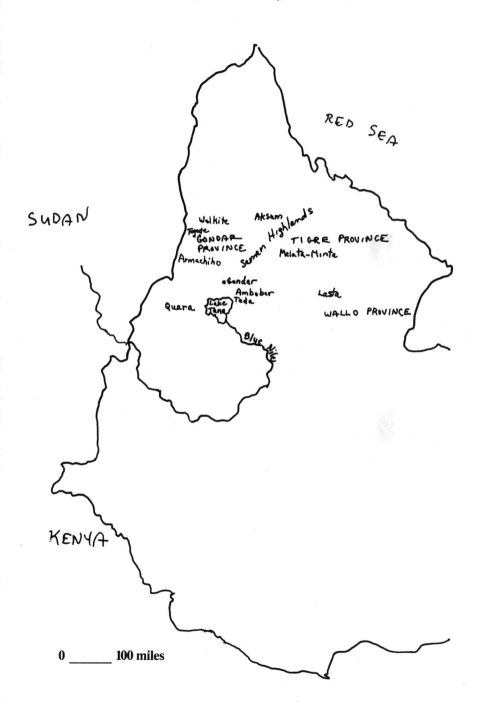

It was late in the winter of 1981. With my friend Yakov, for weeks I had been running from village to village across Ethiopia pursued by agents of the provincial government of Gondar and by *shiftas*—outlaws—who were after the bounty the government had placed on our heads. Finally, in the small hours of the morning, I could see Sudan ahead in the distance. I was more exhausted than my companion; as soon as we stopped, I dropped to the ground and fell into a deep sleep.

I had a dream: the governor's soldiers were chasing us from Gondar province and we were running as fast as we could. We came to the Sudan border, but were confronted by a gorge that was too wide to jump; even attempting it would have been suicide.

On the far side in Sudan, I saw my father standing. He called out, "Okay, take it easy—don't worry, be strong. Things will be all right."

My father carried heavy, flat boards and placed them spanning the gorge. "There's no problem," he yelled across the gorge. "Walk across carefully, and then toss the boards back down."

We did as he said, then he turned and disappeared into Sudan. I chased him, to find and kiss him. But he was gone.

At that time, my father had been dead for over four years. Since his death, I had dreamed about him often when I was in trouble in Ethiopia. But since that night, when we lost each other in Sudan, I rarely dream about him.

It was fitting that I should have dreamed about my father on my last day in the land of my birth. So much had happened to me in the years since I had lived in the small, rural Jewish village where I was born. I was now a grown man with a family of my own—an educated person who had managed to succeed in the urban, Christian-secular society of Ethiopia. Yet everything I had become remained tied to what my father had taught me years before. It was he who had instilled the deep Jewish values that sustained me. Even the fact that I finally had to run from Ethiopia was a result of the strong Jewish identity he had given to me.

My father had been a wise man. Sometimes I wonder whether he would have been shocked by the unpredictable route my life took. I like to think he would have been proud of me.

In these pages I will tell the story of my life. I write as an Ethiopian Jew (we call ourselves *Beta Yisrael* or House of Israel; *Falasha*, which other Ethiopians called us, is a pejorative term meaning "landless one"). Our Ethiopian Jewish heritage is a proud one.

Traditionally, we have had an oral culture. This means that the people of our community shared certain legends, passed by word of mouth from generation to generation. More than thirty years ago, my father forged my connection to our people by recounting for me the tales he had heard from his father.

Because these legends were never written down, it would be easy to dismiss them as inaccurate, but that would be a mistake. There is no reason to assume that what history books record is necessarily more accurate. In an oral culture people become highly skilled at retaining material, so what comes down to us, even across the centuries, may possess a great deal of validity. My own approach has been to balance what I learned as a child against what I have since found in books. Truth can be found in many places.

According to the best-known legend of our origins, we are descended from Menelick I, the son born of Solomon's seduction of the Queen of Sheba. Unfortunately, this was distorted and exploited by Haile Selassie during his long reign as emperor of Ethiopia; Selassie, hoping to establish his descent from the line of Solomon, brazenly called himself the "The Lion of Judah."

There are other stories that recount the beginnings of our people. At the time of the destruction of the First Temple—586 B.C.E.—the Jews were exiled from Jerusalem. "Our" group—the people who later became the Jews of Ethiopia—went in two directions. Some went to Egypt and some to southern Arabia, to what is now Yemen. According to the legend, the Jews who went to Egypt had stayed for many years when Egypt was invaded; the tale as I heard it does not name the invaders, but I imagine they were the Persians who came to Egypt about 525 B.C.E. These Jews, who spoke Aramaic and practiced a prerabbinic form of Judaism (vestiges of which can still be found in our religious practices), were skilled people with services to offer, and they actively cooperated with the foreign rulers.

When the invaders were finally driven out of Egypt, after some two hundred years of occupation, Egyptian anger was turned against the Jews who had cooperated with them. The Jews took their families and fled, following the Blue Nile south, through what is today Sudan, to Lake Tana, the source of the Blue Nile in Ethiopia. In time they moved out into the northern highlands of Ethiopia—Armachiho, Walkite, Tegede, and Quara in Gondar, Lasta in Wollow province, and up to Tigre—and settled in these places.

According to our oral legends, the Jews in Ethiopia then formed a kingdom of considerable size and power and maintained it during a period of history when no other independent Jewish kingdom existed. In its early centuries, the Ethiopian kingdom—known as the Auxumite kingdom—was clearly Semitic with roots that went back to ancient Israel. This, also, is recognized by written history. Even today's Ethiopian Christians accept the fact that Judaism was once the official religion of the land. Precisely because of those strong Jewish roots, Ethiopian Christian practices are still more Jewish than the practices of other Christian sects.

In the fourth century C.E., when the Jewish queen Yehudit ruled much of the land, Christianity finally arrived in Ethiopia. She and her loyal subjects battled the Christians but lost much of their territory and were driven into the highlands. When the conversion to Christianity took place in the kingdom, those Jews who refused to convert were pushed back. At this point, for the first time, there may have been a cooperative effort between the Jews of Ethiopia and the Agaus—an indigenous Ethiopian tribe that had not participated in the Jewish kingdom. Finding themselves both excluded from the newly Christian Auxumite kingdom, they may have moved together against it. If marriages between Jews and Agaus did occur, our tradition makes it clear that stringent conversion to Judaism would have been required first. Even at the time when some Jews in Ethiopia had slaves, those slaves were converted before being brought into Jewish households.

It is also known that there have been links between Ethiopia and Yemen for some two thousand years. The commercial ties were there; bartering across the Red Sea was common. Our legends tell us that at some point there was war between the Christian Ethiopian kingdom and the Jews of Yemen. Jews were taken captive by the Ethiopians, and brought to the northern highlands where the Ethiopian Jews already lived in high concentration. In time, the captive Yemenite population was absorbed into the community.

Historical evidence strongly suggests that this took place in the sixth century C.E., when the Jewish king Yusuf ruled Yemen—then called Himyar—and waged war against Ethiopia. The Yemenite Jews are rabbinic Jews. By this point in history they had the Talmud, the written body of rabbinic Jewish law, and would have brought some of it with them into Ethiopia.

In Semen, in the very area where these two Jewish populations came together fourteen centuries ago, there remains the highest concentration of Ethiopia's Jews. Here, isolated in the highlands, is an ancient Jewish school—Melata-Minata—a training place for *keses*. The *keses-kohanim* in Hebrew—are priests. In the Ethiopian Jewish community there are no rabbis; the religious leadership is modeled after the priesthood of the Temple of ancient Israel.

There was a time when almost every *kes* was trained in Melata-Minata. Today, it is hard to say whether any training at all still goes on. But although the government has closed all other Jewish schools in recent years, it has allowed this religious academy to remain open. Everyone understands that this is a singularly holy place, not to be disturbed. Furthermore, there has never been anything political about Melata-Minata; it has had no association with Zionism, the Jewish Agency, or with American interests. The respect with which it is treated even by those otherwise hostile to Jews is a reflection of its established place in Ethiopian society.

The Ethiopian Coptic Church still possesses a great deal of written material about the ancient roots of the Jews in Ethiopia. Since the time of Gideon, the last Jewish king before the final defeat of the Jewish kingdom by the Christians in the seventeenth century, these writings have been withheld from us. Among the materials hidden are Jewish texts written in Aramaic. In the Auxum area, where the first Ethiopian kingdom was located, there are many volumes—including the Torah—written in Hebrew. *Keses* have traced the location of important religious books and bargained for them with the Christian priests. I, myself, know of three churches where ancient Jewish books are secreted, and during my last year in Ethiopia I was anxious to acquire them at any cost. But negotiations moved too slowly, and by the time of my escape no final agreement had been reached. The books are not being used, but because the church is eager to suppress and rewrite Ethiopian Jewish history, the Coptic priests continue to hide them. Now, with an antireligious Marxist government in Ethiopia, it is likely that these books have been taken from the churches and burned. However, in the northern provinces, where government activity is limited by antigovernment rebels, I am convinced that ancient, holy books are still preserved. Acquiring them today would not be a simple matter—considerable risk and expense would be involved. Yet I believe that it would be possible.

Back as far as the time of Queen Yehudit, in the fourth century, Jewish books were burned. Legends concerning their retrieval are still told today. Once the books were destroyed, learned men of the day sat down to write them over again from memory. In doing so, they incorporated what Hebrew words they remembered. For this reason Jewish versions of certain texts in Ethiopia differ from the Christian versions of the same texts. The Christian versions have no Hebrew, but are written in Ge'ez, an ancient holy tongue of Ethiopia derived from Hebrew. There are other legends which tell of a time some hundreds of years ago when the Ethiopian Jews still spoke Hebrew. Ancient books belonging to my people and written in Hebrew would certainly provide evidence for this.

Although it is no longer spoken, Ge'ez is still the language of Ethiopia's religious liturgy, in much the same way that elsewhere for centuries Hebrew was not spoken by Jews in ordinary conversation but was used for prayer. Ethiopian Jews have the Torah in Ge'ez. Amharic, the language spoken today by most Jews in Ethiopia, is derived from Ge'ez. Tigrenian, spoken in Tigre provence, is closer to Hebrew than Amharic. And as a child I was told that "the old ones" spoke a Jewish language. That language was Quarigna, used only by older Jews who lived in the Quara area. Quarigna is a Semitic tongue, even closer to Hebrew than Ge'ez. The routes taken by the Jews who came down from Egypt explain its origin. Some Jews, following the Blue Nile, crossed into Ethiopia and settled in Quara, where in close community they were able to maintain their traditions. Others, who spread farther out into the highlands, lost more of their original culture as time passed.

There is a common misunderstanding that Ethiopian Jews are "Torah" Jews, meaning that our Jewish practices are guided only by the first five books of the Bible, known as the Torah. This is simply wrong, and does us an injustice. While we do observe the Torah with great devotion, to say that we have only Torah is a distortion that enables scoffers to raise doubts about the legitimacy of our Jewishness. The evidence is clear that we are historically bound to the broader traditions of the Jewish people.

We do not have the written Talmud of the rabbis, because we were already isolated in the Ethiopian highlands before it was written. But we do have traces of oral law— *Torah sh'ba'al peh*—the laws passed by word of mouth that were later recorded in the Talmud. Our observance of this oral law is further proof of our common heritage with Jews the world over. There is, for example, the fact that we wash and say a blessing before and after we eat, which is rabbinic in origin and not written in Torah. Our method of circumcision and of slaughtering animals, and some of our rules about capital punishment, correspond to rabbinic law as well. These practices are all very old and seem to be ones that we have had throughout our history; even the ancient language of the blessings involved indicate that they have been used for centuries. Some of these practices may have been brought to Ethiopia by the Jews of Yemen who joined our ancestors, others may be so ancient that we carried them from an even earlier time.

The great antiquity of our Jewish roots is reflected in the fact that we have priests, as in the days of the Temple, rather than rabbis. We keep Shabbat and all the festivals and are true to the biblical injunction not to seethe a kid in its mother's milk. We observe the laws of *niddah*, which requires the separation of a woman during her menstrual period, with great stringency. (In our villages we maintain a separate hut, called the *mergem-gojo*, where a menstruating woman is confined, usually with several other women. At the end of her stay, she must immerse herself in the *mikvah*—the ritual bath, usually a nearby river—and clean her clothes before entering her house in the evening.)

Brit Milah, ritual circumcision on the eighth day, is a ceremony of great importance for Ethiopian Jews. The mother is already in the *mergem-gojo*, where she must remain for forty days after giving birth. Because she is nursing her child, he stays there with her. At the time of the circumcision, the family and friends gather outside of the hut. Only the *mohel*, who will perform the circumcision, enters the *mergem*. When the mother emerges from her period of ritual impurity, she takes her child into the *mikvah* with her—by virtue of his contact with her, he, too, has become unclean. In the same way, the *mohel*, having touched the child during circumcision, must immerse himself in the *mikvah* before he is considered ritually clean.

This concern with separation and ritual purity is found throughout the practices of our people and reflects the traditional Jewish orientation to life. The French scholar and linguist Joseph HaLevy, who came to Ethiopia in 1867 to investigate the black Jews after rumors of them had been brought to Europe by Christian missionaries, found them living in villages so utterly separate from the rest of the Ethiopian population that anyone even coming into contact with a non-Jew was required to immerse in the *mikvah*.

HaLevy's visit was the beginning of something new for us—it was our first contact with modern rabbinic Judaism. And it was a student of HaLevy's, Jacques Faitlovitch, who had the greatest impact on Ethiopian Jewry. Faitlovitch (1881-1955) devoted his life to the Jews of Ethiopia. He considered them to be true Jews, and believed there was an obligation to bring them into the modern world. He visited in 1904; when he left for Europe, he took with him two Ethiopian Jewish students. Years later, Faitlovitch and his now educated students, Emanuel Tamrat and Eliahu Gete, returned. In Addis Ababa, the capital, Faitlovitch established the first Ethiopian school for Jewish students in 1924. This marked the beginning of important changes; and in a very real sense, it established the direction my life would someday take.

Ethiopia: Provinces
And Major Cities
(Hand-Drawn By The Author)

Saudi
Arabia

Red
Sea

Eritrea

Khartoum

Asmara

Yemen

Hummara
Abderafi
Metema

Tigre

Gondar
Gonder

SIMIEN
MOUNTAINS

Sudan

Lake
Tana

Wallow

Gojam

Debe Arba

Welega

Shewa

ADDIS (6)
ABABA

Somalia

Harerge

Arsi

Ilubabor

ETHIOPIA

Kefa

Bale

Gamo
Gofa

Sidamo

Uganda

Kenya

⊢━━━━┥
150 miles

2

Life in My Village

My father was a special kind of village teacher; he was a bridge between two religious worlds. He had been among the thirty-odd students who were the first graduates of the Jewish school opened in Addis Ababa by Faitlovitch. The majority of the young men in that class returned to their own villages, bringing what they had learned to their communities. Their teachings represented the start of formal rabbinic education for the Jews of Ethiopia.

I was born in a village near the city of Gondar, where my father taught. It was a small town, barely thirty or forty families in all. By the time I was old enough to know what was happening, my father had already been teaching for some years, but I am told that he had quite a struggle in the beginning. There was no schoolhouse and there were certainly no supplies; the children studied either under a tree or in my father's house. Faitlovitch had arranged for my father to receive a modest salary, but some time passed before it came with with any regularity. In order to support his family, my father worked as a sharecropper as well as a teacher.

When I began my formal studies, it was my father who taught me. From him I learned such general skills as math and reading and writing in Amharic. We spent time on Jewish subjects as well; I studied the Hebrew alphabet, Jewish ethics, and rabbinic Judaism. He always referred to his teacher, Emanuel Tamrat, who had been one of Faitlovitch's European-educated disciples.

My father never differentiated Ethiopian Judaism from rabbinic Judaism. He never told me, "This is what we have traditionally done, and this is what I have learned others do." He taught me this way: "*Hakadosh, boruch hu, natan Torah* [The Holy One, blessed be He, gave Torah] ... and from Torah we learn to do this and this." He told me that we had no right to amend law which had come from Jerusalem: "And when you come next year to Jerusalem, you will have to accept the laws as they are." I suspect that in his wisdom he foresaw many things.

Life in my village, as in all the villages, was communal. The houses were round straw huts, called *tukuls*. The people depended mostly on agriculture, although the women also made pottery and spun while the men wove and worked metal. The pottery, cloth, and metalwork were made both for personal use and for sale.

The houses were circular; a large family might have a *tukul* of forty or fifty square meters. Inside every *tukul* were large circular mud and grass containers, called *gotahs*— roughly two or two and a half meters high—used to store grain. These containers were quite important to us. First, of course, because they kept the grain safe and dry, but also because money and other valuables, including weapons, were safely hidden in them, buried under the grain. These *gotahs* had additional use because they were lined up across one side of the house, sometimes five or more in a row, to form a wall of sorts. In another part of the *tukul*, a piece of cloth or leather might be hung as a curtain for privacy as well.

Parents had an area to themselves, but when guests came, room was always provided. Within our culture, no one is ever turned away. Weather permitting, a guest might sleep outside; otherwise space is made available inside the *tukul*. The bed traditionally consists of a wooden platform, cushioned with grass or other soft material and covered with leather. In our home we had European metal beds, left behind by the Italian forces that occupied Ethiopia during World War II. If there is not enough room for guests, the children must go next door to sleep at a neighbor's. This communal style of living affects how we relate to one another; we develop a need for having others around, and for the comfort that comes with touch. No doubt much of this is foreign to the urbanized, wealthy West, which values privacy above all.

Until the age of seven, children were not given any formal education, but girls learned essential skills from their mothers, boys from their fathers. When a father went to the field to work, his son would go along to watch. By watching, he would learn what to do.

Ethiopian Jews in the villages believed that children are a kind of wealth, for children are the source of power and income. More children meant more family members at work. It was the responsibility of the father to instruct his sons to be hard-working men.

Within the Ethiopian Jewish family there is a kind of formalized respect not well understood in the West. At mealtimes, for example, when I was growing up, the parents would eat first; the children later. As the meal began, it was the responsibility of the eldest son to assist his father in washing his hands, when the traditional blessing was said. Then he would stand holding a candle throughout the meal. The other sons would stand as well while the daughters could sit. At the end of the meal, the father would give a piece of whatever he had been eating to his eldest son first, as a sign that he had done well. Then something was given to each of the other sons, according to age.

A family's sons stay within the household. When a young man marries, his wife leaves her family and joins his. She is considered, in all respects, a part of the new family. The young couple has separate sleeping quarters; the husband builds a mini-*tukul*, nearby or attached to his parents'. In all other ways, they remain part of the parents' household.

The time for a couple to leave the parents' home comes when their first child is born; this is a significant event in our society. The son who has produced his own child is considered to have earned a new status. He builds his own separate *tukul* and becomes his father's neighbor. He may continue to farm with his father, or his father may give a part of the land he rents to his son. When the couple first married, it is likely that the husband received a dowry from the wife's father, often firearms. Now, as the new household is formed, both fathers may contribute something more to it.

In some areas, long ago, as a protection against assimilation, girls were taken as wives when still very young, although there would be no sexual relations between the couple until the girl matured. The father of a young boy would go into another village and find the girl he wanted for his son. He would give a token sum to the girl's father to seal the bargain. If it could be arranged, when she was between the ages of seven and twelve, she would come to live in the boy's household. This was a difficult transition for a child: a new household, a new village, a new environment. But in time she might forget her original family and come to think of this new family as her own.

The most difficult adjustment came when the couple was required to sleep together for the first time, since by then they may have begun to think of each other as brother and sister. At this point a great deal depended on the sensitivity of the boy's parents. If the mother advised the girl, and the father instructed the son, then it would be easier. But the transition was nevertheless made, and in time a new household would be established.

The staple food of the Jews of Ethiopia, as of all Ethiopians, is *injerra*, a fermented, pancakelike bread made of the grain *tef*, and *wot*, a stew made with a spicy sauce.

There is also ordinary bread. Traditionally, grain was ground by hand, but now it is sometimes brought to the city to be done. On Shabbat there is a special bread, *berkete*, eaten during the day. In the days when food was plentiful, rich families might have slaughtered a sheep before every Shabbat.

How much food was available depended very much on the region. If the area was fertile, even though the Jews could not own land, they might have managed well. In addition, the Jews were skilled at the handicrafts that developed into cottage industries: pottery, weaving, and so forth. Communities farther out from the city tended to be wealthier, because the level of consumption was lower.

There was a time when all Jews had enough food; the Jews of Ethiopia were not always the poorest of the poor. Even recently, when things first became more difficult and such items as clothing were in short supply, the Jews were hungry, but not yet dying of starvation. Now, however, this is no longer the case: word has come from Ethiopia of Jews who are literally starving.

The celebration of Shabbat and festivals in a Ethiopian Jewish village is different from that of Israel because of its intensely communal nature. All members of the community, young and old alike, except for those who are ritually unclean, go to the synagogue compound. The men and older women go into the synagogue; there is no physical barrier between them, but they do not touch. The younger women stay in the courtyard and listen from there.

The *kes* is the leader of the synagogue, the *dabtara* his helper. Prayers are read by the *kes* in Ge'ez; the *dabtara* translates into Amharic, the language everyone understands. There is, of course, Torah reading as well, done in Ge'ez with an Amharic translation, and preaching by the *kes*, usually a homily related to the weekly Torah reading.

Besides the Torah, we have the other books of the Bible and additional writings in Ge'ez: Enoch, the Book of Angels, Te'ezaza Sanbat (the Precepts of Shabbat), the Testament of Abraham, the Death of Moses. All of these are read in the synagogue on different occasions and incorporated into the preaching.

After the Shabbat prayers are complete, food is brought to a communal area and everyone eats together. Food is cold; we keep no fires on Shabbat. In some areas, the meal includes a rabbinic introduction, the *kiddush*, a blessing over wine.

The *kes* of a village is looked upon as leader, mediator, and judge; he commands great respect. The community supports him by supplying labor for his fields so that he does not have to engage in manual labor. If his harvest is not sufficient, others will share theirs with him. The people believe that he should receive the best part of everything; even when the Shabbat bread—the *berekete*—is cut, he gets the thickest and best part of it.

We also have a chief priest, a *Kohain Gadol*, nominated by the *keses* from among their own, on the basis of service and knowledge. His role is mostly honorary. The position of *Kohain Gadol* is roughly analagous to that of the chief rabbi of the Israeli rabbinate, but the differences are many.

Ethiopian Jews have always used a lunar calendar that differs markedly from the Ethiopian calendar, but corresponds very closely to the rabbinic Jewish calendar.

Each week, of course, there is *Sanbat* (Shabbat); then

we have *Lenegeta Sanbat*—the seventh Shabbat, or Shabbat of Shabbats—"The Remembrance of Abraham." The tenth day is Yom Kippur, which is called *Asteray*, "The Day for Seeking Pardon," and it is a day of fasting and prayer, as everywhere else in the Jewish world.

We celebrate Sukkot and call it *Bale Metselet*. In my village every home had a *sukkah*, or *dass*. The ritual use of the *lulov* and *etrog* was not part of our tradition and was introduced into Ethiopia by rabbis in recent times.

Passover or *Fassika* is a holiday of tremendous importance to us. Observance is very strict. For example, the use of dairy products is frowned on, because they may ferment. Houses are thoroughly cleaned and all leavening put aside days before the holiday begins. Since our contact with Faitlovitch, the people no longer perform the Pascal sacrifice; but there is often fasting until sundown on Passover Eve, when a lamb is slaughtered and there is feasting and an oral recounting of Exodus.

Shavuot or *Mirer* is observed and is known as a family visitation day. Rich families within the village often invite everyone to celebrate with them at a communal meal.

We observed Purim in Ethiopia, although there seems to be a mistaken impression that we did not. We had the *Megillat Ester*, the Book of Esther. We fasted and read the *Megillah*, but we believed the celebration should be saved for Jerusalem. We did not dress up or decorate things the way Jews do elsewhere.

The holiday that did not reach us, because it was established by the rabbis at a late date, is Chanukah. The fact is that our ancestors had left Israel before the time of the Maccabees in the Second Century B.C.E.

Seg'd is an ancient holiday that no other Jewish community celebrates any longer. It is a little earlier in the year than Chanukah, but has no connection with it. After the destruction of the First Temple, the Jews dispersed in Persia wanted to return. They climbed a mountain, faced Jerusalem, and prayed to be allowed to go back to the holy city. In ancient times the whole Jewish world was aware of this practice, but only the Ethiopian Jews have continued to keep it. For the past few years, Ethiopian Jews in Israel have celebrated the *Seg'd* at the Western Wall in Jerusalem, praying for all of our people to join us; but I believe the ceremony will ultimately lose its significance here.

In my day, it was difficult for Ethiopian Jews to get a secular education. Even where education was locally available, Jewish families did not send their children to government schools because they feared assimilation. Today they are still wary and not without reason.

If they did send their children away to school, it was almost always the boys who went. Girls were believed to be too vulnerable: either they wouldn't come back at all, or they would come back pregnant. Even when formal Jewish study started to become a possibility—first in Addis and then in Europe—only boys were sent. This created a problem, for as boys began to be educated, they were unable to find educated Jewish girls. Since they were reluctant to take wives who had not studied, they were pushed ever further into assimilation.

In my mother's family, no one had a formal education, so it wasn't surprising that she didn't want me to go to government schools. However, my father did; he was in favor of secular as well as religious education. My mother refused, and a major dispute erupted between my parents. My mother wanted me to marry a girl from the village and live the kind of life her family had always known; she saw no need for change. But I was encouraged by my father and by his brothers.

My father's views prevailed.

When I finally went to a government school, I was registered as a *Beta Yisrael*, openly identifying as a Jew. I walked over fourteen kilometers a day, without shoes; there were other Jews from nearby villages who walked even farther than I. By then I was fourteen, old enough to understand what was good and what was bad.

When I returned home from school each day I had to help my older, married brother with the family farming. My father, occupied with his teaching, had little time to devote to it. Our method of farming is what would be referred to as "primitive," and it was hard work.

The school I attended was a provincial school. With the basic training my father had given me, I was able to enter at the third grade. It took me four years to complete elementary school through the eighth grade. From the fourth grade up, classes were taught in English by British and Indian teachers. The standards were extremely high then, although that is no longer the case today. By the seventh grade, my teachers were American Peace Corps volunteers.

At the end of the eighth grade, I took an exam to qualify for a comprehensive high school in the city of Gondar. I received a high grade and entered a school for boys. It was very difficult for me, as a Jew, to come together with non-Jews in that community. They called me *buda*, "evil-eye," a common anti-Semitic epithet in Ethiopia, and harrassed me constantly. Yet all of this motivated me: I felt challenged to become superior by learning more than the others.

Although I was a good student, I had financial problems. I needed more than I had in order to look like my fellow classmates, who were rich. I don't believe my father was a poor man at that time, but my mother didn't understand my situation or know what kind of material competition I faced. She felt that if she gave me too much, she would spoil me. So, while the others had shoes, I did not, and I wore short pants while they had long trousers.

Then help came from an unexpected source. The government decided that every student who received more than 60 percent on the eighth-grade exam would receive a monthly stipend as long as he attended high school. For someone living in the same district as the high school, the amount was ten birr (there are approximately two Ethiopian birr to the American dollar) and for someone in a far district, fifteen.

The Peace Corps volunteers who were my teachers were very fond of me because I was a serious and cooperative student. They, too, sought to help me. I had no special skills, but they found me a job anyway, sending me once a week to work with the man who tended their horses. For this I was paid fifteen birr.

In all, I had twenty-five birr, which was a lot of money to me. I would take one birr and buy a kilo of fresh *buna*—coffee—and bring it to my mother, along with the rest of the money. Then I'd ask my parents for a small sum in order to buy school materials: exercise books, pencils, and so forth. Getting money for clothes was a different matter. I certainly asked. "We haven't anything to give you," I was told. "You have enough." I didn't argue although it would never have occurred to me to keep even a part of the twenty-five birr which I'd received. I was not only showing my parents respect, I was trying to convince my mother that, even though I was in school, I was nonetheless productive. It was my hope that she would come to see my education as a good thing.

I kept my job until the tenth grade and then I simply couldn't handle it anymore; the schoolwork had become too demanding. I had a long walk every day and no electricity for studying at night. That's when I started cheating on Shabbat. Since even reading schoolwork was forbidden on

Shabbat, I would go out of my house to a place where I could not be seen. I never wrote on Shabbat, but I reasoned that if it was all right to read the Bible, it would also be all right to read a science book.

My father caught me once, but he wasn't the kind of man to use a beating as punishment; he gave me advice, explaining the consequences of my behavior: "Once or twice you can cheat, but ultimately you will be caught. You cannot hide from God."

In ninth grade there was an incident that made a big impression on me and would have repercussions later in my life. I got into trouble with a non-Jewish classmate, a boy who grew up to be an administrator of Gondar province, and who even then had a reputation as an anti-Semite. Many Ethiopian Jews tell stories of their arrests when they tried to escape from Ethiopia. This boy, Tefera Melaku, later emerged as the official who would supervise their torture.

He sat next to me in school. Although two or three years older, he was short, and so was placed up front with me. He came from a distant district without a high school and lived in a rented house; his family was very rich. Even at that age, he drank and frequented the area where the prostitutes lived, because he could get *kirari* beer there. When he came to class, he smelled. His nickname became Melaku Kirari.

One day we had a math exam and Melaku, knowing that I was prepared and he was not, asked if he could copy my paper. I remember thinking that he really had no excuse because he'd come from a city with electrity for studying at night, but I reluctantly agreed. However, the examiner, a big tall American man, was standing beside us. I finished my work, stood up, and handed the examiner the paper without letting Melaku cheat. Then I ran out of the room.

The next day we got our exams back. I had a perfect score; he got 25 percent. He was angry and called me *buda.* "I studied," he said to me, "but you had the evil eye, and you took it from me." That is the way anti-Semites in Ethiopia think; I'm sure it's the way he was taught.

I was very angry, lost control, and slapped him. He was quite strong, but as he got up to come at me, he tripped and fell. A teacher saw this, and blamed me. I was punished, which seemed a terrible injustice to me. Three days later, unable to bear how I was feeling any longer, I hit him again, this time with a stone hidden in my fist. Ultimately, it became necessary for my father to intervene and the situation quieted down.

In the years following, Melaku did not do well. I ran into him when I was at the university. He was taking a one-year preparatory course, but did not succeed at it. Then, with his father's influence, he was sent to a military academy. After he graduated, he came back to Addis and was appointed bodyguard for His Imperial Majesty, Haile Selassie. Over the years, we occasionally met and were always superficially friendly. He even joked about what had happened years before, but I knew that he was not the sort of person to really let go of his anger.

At the end of the tenth grade, because my achievement level was high, I was allowed to sit for qualifying exams. If I passed, I could move on to one of a number of different schools—teacher training school, technical college, agricultural school, and so forth. These were four-year schools, which meant that I would have gone through eleventh and twelfth grade and then studied for two years beyond that.

My teachers tried to find a way to send me to an educational program in America, known as the Field Service Program. This was a one-year program for twelfth graders, who would complete high school in the United States and then sit for a qualifying exam for university. I was only in the tenth grade, but my teachers felt that I was competent enough to succeed and encouraged me to try.

So I sat for the exam and passed, but the rules stipulated that parents would have to pay half the expenses, some 540 birr, and I had no access to that kind of money. My teachers contributed half, but there was still no way for me to find the balance. Finally, my math teacher agreed to pay everything and I was ready to go.

However, a student of Faitlovitch's had recently died in the United States. He had been sent by Haile Selassie's government to study there. Since that time, I have heard that he committed suicide in America, but then it was said that he had been killed. He had been special—a sensitive person who worked for the Jews—and my father had loved him. Everyone was very upset by the news of his death and my mother cried and said that if I went to America, she would die.

My mother told me that if I went to Addis Ababa to study, she would not mind so much because I had uncles not far away. But I had no one in the United States. "Haile Selassie killed one student there because he was Jewish," she said. "If you go to the United States, I will die first, because you will die there."

That ended my plan to study in the United States. Still, it was the first time I'd heard from my mother that it would be all right with her if I went to Addis to study. So I sat for the exams for that and passed.

At that time my father had calves and goats and more, but he did not have cash. He had nothing to give me. I borrowed five birr, which is what it cost to get to the school I had selected, and I went.

3

Beyond
the
Village

The first year I boarded at the technical school was a hard one for me. I was the only Jew there, and I had never been away from my mother before. I had never eaten food prepared by others, not even bread. Now I was served flesh prepared by Christians and improperly slaughtered. For a whole year the sight of it made me sick. In Ethiopian Christian culture, Wednesdays and Fridays are meatless—I loved them. On those days I ate, even though I knew the food wasn't strictly kosher; I was learning to compromise for the sake of education.

The government provided me with food, working clothes, and soap for those clothes. For the first time I had a pair of shoes—made of plastic—bought for me by one of my uncles. But there remained the problem of other clothes; I needed more than shoes.

I wrote to another uncle and was sent fifteen birr. I returned the five birr I had borrowed to get to school, and spent the remaining money on a haircut, toiletries, and other things I needed. The ten birr was soon gone, and I knew I would have to find ways to help myself.

Six of us lived together in one big dormitory room with three double beds. My roommates were from rich families in Wolleka, coffee producers and distributors. They were lazy, always sleeping or going out. I never got the chance to go anywhere except to classes, the library, the laboratory or back to my room; without money, there was nowhere else for me to go. My roommates knew I had extra time, and offered to pay me to wash their clothes. With this work, I earned a total of twenty-five birr—this was big money and it was all mine.

Two of the other boys in my room were in the same department of study as me. The richer of them never did his homework. So I began doing his assignments for him as well as my own, and when he went home for vacation, he bought me the clothes I needed out of the money I had earned.

When I went home for vacation, I brought what was left of my money and gave it to my parents. But my mother drank a lot of coffee, which was very expensive, and between the cost of coffee and sugar, the money was quickly gone.

The first year my studies did not go well. I was sick because I had picked up an intestinal parasite from the drinking water. The second year went better; my health improved and I started eating, even though the food was not kosher. I had gone to visit my uncles and had seen that they were buying meat from a non-kosher market. When I returned to school, I began to eat it too. I didn't actually chew the meat at first—I couldn't actually bring myself to—but I ate the sauce it was cooked in. By my third year of school I was a bit spoiled; I ate the meat.

In my first year, I had studied in the agromechanics department, learning about farms and tractors. The department had fields that were used for teaching; but, incredibly, despite the fact that they were fertile, no one planted them. They were plowed by the students—made ready for planting—and then left fallow.

I had come from a hard-working family. So I went to the director of the school and asked him if I could use the field myself.

"For what?" he asked.

"To plant it."

"What will you plant?"

I told him I wasn't sure.

"Well," he said, "plant vegetables. I'll get the kitchen manager to buy what you grow."

So, for perhaps two birr, I bought a variety of seeds. The director got me some plastic hosing for watering them so I didn't even have to carry water. He liked me, but didn't know I was Jewish. All he knew was that I was poor.

My classmates, who knew I was Jewish, respected me nonetheless, despite my inability to compete with them in things like clothing. But I still felt a terrible loneliness among the Christians. Our interactions tended to be superficial; we held a lot inside ourselves. However, the education I got was of high quality—and that, after all, was my reason for being there. I worked hard and kept to myself.

What was most difficult was for me to keep my Jewishness alive while separated from my parents by hundreds of kilometers. In the beginning, although I had no Jewish calendar, I was nevertheless aware of the Jewish holidays. But there was no way for me to leave my studies and go back home for them. After a while, I began to lose track of the holidays themselves, and I struggled with terrible guilt over this; my Jewish commitment was still very strong.

After four years, I finished at the technical school. At the time of my graduation, I signed a contract with the government. I had been provided with a free education and four years of residence at a boarding school. The understanding was that if the government had need of me, I would have to serve wherever they chose. I stood fourth in my graduating class and first in my department; the Ministry of Education took the four top students in the class to be teachers in comprehensive high schools. I did not like it—the pay was poor and teachers had little social status—but I had no choice.

I was required to attend educational workshops at the university for two months during the summer for a program called Teacher Core. Canadian and American teachers taught the courses, which were scheduled to extend over five consecutive summers.

About this time, I became aware of a scholarship being offered for study in the Soviet Union. This interested me quite a bit, not because of the socialist ideology—I knew little of that and did not care—I was simply eager to study out of the country, especially since I had lost my chance to go to the United States earlier.

However, once again things stood in my way: my commitment to the government and my obligation to my parents. I had been raised to believe that it is the parents' duty to help their children until they are grown; then it is the children's responsibility to assist their parents, especially as they begin to grow older.

By Western standards, perhaps, the amount of assistance my parents had given me was small; I'd helped myself and educated myself a good deal. But that didn't matter—they had helped me, and I'd received the motivation to study from my father. Moreover, during the years I was at school, I had not been helping with the farm work at home, and my parents had thereby suffered a loss of income. I realized that I wouldn't have any peace with myself unless I gave my parents a large sum of money to pay them back.

What I finally decided was to escape from my obligation to the government, and find well-paid work, so I could repay my parents. During the summer, while studying the methodology of teaching at the university, I was careful not to accept any government money, which would have increased my obligation. I believed that after I had repaid my parents, I would be able to leave the country for higher education. It never occurred to me that in order to apply for a foreign scholarship, I would have to work through the Ministry of Education.

Secretly, I left Addis Ababa and went far away, to Eritrea province. The Ministry of Education didn't know where I was and the government wasn't well enough organized to find me. I didn't even have to change my name. I simply became lost in another part of a big country.

In Eritrea, I found a well-paying job at an oil refinery. If I had stayed in Addis, the Ministry of Education would have paid me 350 birr a month; now I was netting 600. From this, I sent 300 or 400 birr to my parents each month. I wanted them to buy back some of the things they had sold over the past few years. My brother's family was large and they'd needed cash so badly that my father had even been compelled to sell his firearms.

For seven months, I worked in Eritrea, but I developed an asthmatic condition there and had to leave. I went to visit my parents and found that nothing had changed in my village. My parents were glad that I was succeeding and had been supporting them. On the holidays, they gave large celebrations to show their gratitude to God and invited people from the neighboring villages. But it was my money they used for these religious celebrations. They had given no thought to their material welfare and had replaced none of the things they had lost over the years.

I had made an agreement with my parents. I asked

them where the oxen and cows they had promised to buy back were. They told me that what they were doing with the money was the easiest and best thing for them. I accepted it; but I also knew that since they had not replaced their goods they would find it more and more difficult to survive independently in the future, and that it would become harder and harder for me to leave the country.

"You don't want me to go to learn?" I asked them.

"That's not important anymore," they said. "We are growing old. We don't know when we'll die. If you go out of the country, you won't see us any more."

I had to change my plans; I knew that I would not go. Because of my health, I couldn't work at the oil refinery any longer. So I had to find another job. I went back to Addis Ababa to look for work, checking the newspaper notices for employment. The electric company was looking for technologists. I went, took an exam, and passed. They offered me a job far from Addis; I wasn't happy about that because I had decided to continue my education there. They said that if I took the job they would bring me back to work in the city in a year's time. I agreed.

I was walking the streets of Addis, thinking about my new job, when someone from the Ministry of Eduction noticed me. He called the police; they came and arrested me. I said I would teach. I had no choice, but because I agreed and had not taken any government money, I was released from jail within twenty-four hours. (Those who had accepted money—I was not the only one who escaped from a teaching assignment—were jailed for a month.)

For one year, I taught tenth grade math in a high school in a southern province, with Peace Corps volunteers. The following summer, I returned to Addis to continue my teaching courses. I completed them four years later.

During that first year of teaching, I was befriended by

a man who had a significant impact on me. He was a fat American Jew, head of the math department, and he became my mentor. In one summer I had not learned much educational methodology; I was without practical experience. This man showed me what to do, so that I knew how to present my material and prepare lessons. Working alongside him, I learned to love my profession.

I was alone in a new province, with no one I felt I could be close to except him. Because he had told me that he was a Jew, I said that I was also Jewish. He did not believe me. Until I had started to talk about my people, he had never heard of the black Jews of Ethiopia. It hurt me to realize that he thought I was lying. He didn't know me at all. Still, at a professional level we remained close, and I reminded myself that he was an assimilated Jew—his wife, a skinny lady who taught biology, wasn't Jewish.

Others at the school knew I was Jewish—former classmates of mine from Addis came to the area every so often and identified me. It never bothered me; if there was anti-Semitism, it was not openly expressed. However, in that province there was no way for me to practice my religion. All I had was my Jewish feeling. I prayed a lot, although there was no synagogue. I was a single man alone in a single room in a non-Jewish environment.

At the end of the first year every high school teacher in the province was let go. The provincial administrator, an idiot, had made political charges without substance. I was transferred to another province, very far away, but I refused to go. "I'm not a foreign agent," I said. "I can't be kicked out in twenty-four hours this way." Every one of the other teachers responded the same way. On my friend's advice, I had joined the teachers' association, which fought the provincial administrator's decision and, within two months, won.

Government policy at that time did not allow teachers to transfer to Addis Ababa until after they'd had seven years of experience. However, as compensation, I was permitted to go to Addis earlier and became a tenth and eleventh grade math and physics teacher in a comprehensive high school. In time, I assumed administrative duties as well, first for one high school and then for a number of other schools in the region. I began to develop a reputation as an educator.

By this time I was married and had a family, but my situation in earlier years had been difficult: a serious problem of assimilation had confronted me. As long as I had been in my father's house there was no real possibility of assimilation—the influence of family was too strong. However, the seeds were planted even then. In secular school, I learned a new language and opened myself to a variety of cultures; I began to admire some of the teachers and to want to be like them. I found many of the things I saw— such as clothing styles—attractive, but until tenth grade there was no possibility for me to change the way I dressed. What I had was an enormous motivation to go on studying; in my mind learning and change were connected.

Then, greatly determined to be part of the modern world, I went to another province for technical school. I valued study and language and the things of the world that I had learned, and I wanted a Jewish wife. But I couldn't see myself with a village girl who only knew how to sew and cook, who wouldn't be able to understand the things that mattered to me or to share them with me.

Nevertheless, while in technical school, I found a Jewish girl who agreed to be my wife. She was studying in the high school I had just left, itself a rare thing: there were very few educated Jewish girls. Her father, like mine, had been a student of Faitlovitch's, and he and my father were friends. I told my father about our plan to marry and he told her's. They were both pleased and gave their blessings. They knew we were modern, educated young people and they understood it was important for us to agree to our marriage.

But our mothers had not been consulted. And, as it turned out, this girl and I were fifth-generation cousins on our mothers' side. It's a rule of Ethiopian culture–not Jewish culture, just Ethiopian–that there can be no marriages between relatives going back seven generations.

When our mothers found out what our plans were, they were shocked. My mother's brother wrote me a letter, saying that if I married this girl, our children would be dogs, and he visited the worst possible curses upon my future. I felt sick, and broke off with the girl; I had nothing more to do with her.

Then I went to the university, farther away from my family and closer to non-Jewish society. There I fell in love with a non-Jewish girl. What my father had taught was instilled deep within me; I hadn't forgotten my Jewish values. And yet, I was a grown man, a long way from home. I was part of a new environment with a new set of values. I felt free and sophisticated, and in need of female companionship. I told myself that my relationship with her would be temporary.

When my girlfriend became pregnant, I was faced with a decision. However, I wouldn't use her and then dismiss her; she was a human being with a value equal to my own. We decided to marry.

It was important to me that my wife and family be Jewish, and my girlfriend understood that–we had talked about these things. With her I had certainly identified as a Jew, and had always felt that she accepted me for what I was. We agreed that a Jewish home would be important to any future we would have together. She was properly converted under the strict instruction of a *kes*, and our children–three sons–are Jewish children with a strong Jewish identity. Maybe I was lucky; perhaps the strength of the Jewish values my father imparted to me made the difference.

In 1974, Haile Selassie was overthrown in a violent coup, and the revolutionary Marxist regime of Hailu Mengistu Mariam took over the rule of Ethiopia. Political unrest had been the order of the day for some time before the revolution occurred; once it took place the nation was in for a considerable period of further turmoil. Antirevolutionary groups formed and civil war raged in parts of the country.

No aspect of Ethiopian life was untouched and the quality of education was seriously affected. Not long after I had started teaching in Addis Ababa I had to contend with this political and social unrest. Students stayed out of school for strikes and speeches. Teaching stopped being the pleasure it had been. I began to work only part time and to study further in technology.

By late 1978, Ethiopia was approaching the time of "Red Terror," when an uneasy political regime began to take extreme measures. Because of antigovernment activity in Addis Ababa all intellectuals became suspect. Teachers and university students alike were rounded up and put in prison.

Before I knew what was happening, they had come for me. I was handled roughly and no one was willing to answer any questions. I was overwhelmed with a terrifying feeling of helplessness. I knew that I was innocent; no one had ever made any specific charges against me. It reminded me of the time I had been thrown out of my teaching job for no good reason. That, too, was political nonsense, but this was a great deal more serious: I stood to lose my life.

If I had been arrested in Gondar province, I might have been killed. The situation there was worse, and more blatantly anti-Semitic. Only later did I realize how lucky I was to have been in Addis Ababa; at least I had not been jailed because I was a Jew. And medical treatment, not provided in Gondar, was available.

The medical treatment was given for injuries that were the result of torture. The prison administration in Addis followed an interesting procedure: they tortured us until we were in agony, hospitalized us so that we would not die, and then brought us back for additional torture. A common technique involved damaging our feet so that we couldn't escape. I know of one man who had the skin ripped from his soles and was left in his cell until his feet were gangrenous. I know of another who is missing toes.

Other forms of torture were also employed. It wasn't unusual for the guards to hang a man by his wrists from the ceiling and then to beat him across the back. On occasion, someone treated this way would have his wrists so severely fractured that he would have to depend on other prisoners to feed him. I was repeatedly beaten and had an electric wire used on me. There was psychological torture as well: questions shouted repeatedly, threats, and intimidations.

The prison was crowded and filthy. In order to keep strong and divert myself from my misery, I did a lot of exercises in my cell. But I also spent a lot of time sitting and thinking—about my situation, my wife and children, and my father.

When I had been in prison about seven months, I had one of the dreams about my father that came to me every so often. This one has left a particularly strong impression on me.

With wings like a large bird, my father came out of the sky, searching for me. I was trapped in a small hole in the ground that was sealed with a large flat stone over it. He found the hole and lifted the stone. Then he peered in and called to me.

"Yes?" I asked.

"I have come to suffer instead of you," he said.

He sent a rope down and pulled me out. At first, he stood on the ground outside the hole, but as the rope rose up I saw that he was moving up into the air. Finally, I was out of the hole.

From above me, he said, "Close it hard."

I closed it.

He said, "Check it, again."

I checked the hole.

"Is it all right?" he asked.

"All right," I told him.

"Goodbye," he said, and disappeared into the sky.

Out of my sleep, in the prison, I cried out so loudly that friends who were arrested with me heard me and woke me up; my eyes were full of tears.

Four days later, my name was called over the prison loudspeaker. No one else's name was called. When I was led out of my cell, I was sure that I was about to be killed. Instead, I was taken to the prison office and told that I was to be released.

After my release, I returned to my studies.

4

*Jewish
Education
for
The People*

Jewish education in Ethiopia is not a recent innovation. Through the centuries, it has been an intrinsic part of the culture, parents instructing children in Jewish values, history, and rituals. Formal Jewish education in my native land, however, has a more recent and rather shaky history. It began with Faitlovitch's teacher-training school in Addis Ababa in the 1920s. During the early years, Faitlovitch worked with the two Ethiopians he had taken to Europe in 1904: Emanuel Tamrat, who became the director of a school in Addis Ababa, and Eliahu Gete, who was sent into the Gondar area to supervise teachers when they returned to the villages. Faitlovitch even wrote a book in Ge'ez to introduce Eliahu to the people. "Please receive your son as an administrator. He is meant for you, to help you," it said. Eliahu carried it with him.

Faitlovitch's primary goal was to get the people to understand the meaning and content of rabbinic Judaism; he did not emphasize language. There were courses in Hebrew offered in Addis Ababa, but too few of them. His students knew how to read and write Hebrew, but they did not have the understanding necessary to allow them to teach it.

Faitlovitch sent a second group of students out of the country for study. Most of these students never came back to work among the people as he'd hoped they would. They were already too sophisticated, too far away from village life. But one of them, Noah Mandefro, turned out to be a notable exception in terms of his willingness to work with his people. He returned to Ethiopia fluent in European languages and highly educated.

During World War II, all Jewish education in Ethiopia came to a standstill, and Faitlovitch himself left the country. Emanuel did the same; he went with the emperor, Haile Selassie, to London. When Faitlovitch returned to Ethiopia after the war and tried to renew his village education projects, he found that many of the books had been lost. Worse, some of the trained teachers had died, Eliahu among them. Emanuel returned with the emperor; but instead of resuming his Jewish teaching, he went to work as a chargé d'affaires, involving himself with the political issue of the federation of Eritrea. Noah Mandefro was employed by the secular Ministry of Education. Under these conditions, it was impossible for Faitlovitch to develop his programs along the lines he had planned.

Finally, however, Faitlovitch successfully prevailed on Noah to become an administrator of Jewish education in cooperation with the Jewish Agency. In fact, Faitlovitch gathered the *keses* from all the major villages and sent them to a school opened as a teacher-training center in Asmara, in Eritrea, where there was a well-developed rabbinic community. Noah went there to teach, along with rabbis sent from outside and Yemenite Jews from the area. At this school the *keses* were briefed on modern Judaism and given certificates. Most accepted this training in a positive way, although the *kohaim gadol* of Tigre province rejected the idea and returned home.

There were also youngsters at Asmara who were being prepared to go to Kfar Batya in Israel for training, under the sponsorship of Mizrachi Women. Noah, who was responsible for their selection, chose thirty or so during 1955 and

1956. Coming primarily from Gondar and Ambober, these youngsters were in Asmara at the same time as their elders, but their classes were held separately.

The Jewish Agency's Department of Diaspora Jewry supported the Asmara project, providing both funds and personnel. For me, this sort of participation by the Jewish Agency was proof that the Israelis had always known we were Jewish, although some of Israel's policies regarding Ethiopian Jews made it seem otherwise.

When I was teaching high school in Addis, I had some Jewish students who were later hired by Noah as teachers. When Noah was able to get the budget to cover their salaries, he sent them back to their villages to teach their own people. That budget was covered, at least, in part, by the Jewish Agency and I knew it.

But I had other Jewish students who wanted to make *aliyah*, that is, to emigrate to Israel. They filed papers and paid money, but encountered stiff opposition – not from the Ethiopian government, but from the Israeli embassy. (The Israeli Law of Return was not extended officially to apply to Ethiopian Jews until 1975.)

I went to the embassy and saw the ambassador, Hanan Aynor, for the first time. "What kind of people are you?" I asked him. "You send money to educate us as Jews, so you must believe we are Jewish. Yet, while you allow Ethiopian Christians to visit Jerusalem, we are not even permitted tourist visas as Jews."

Aynor tried to evade the issue. He claimed that the educational budget was the Jewish Agency's business, not his; he was an employee of the Ministry of Foreign Affairs and followed its policy. I did not believe him, and pressed on; I found the whole thing rather hard to accept. Aynor finally relented and allowed me to pick three students, and I took the ones who had made the greatest effort, becoming their

guarantor. After that the ambassador started sending me
The Jerusalem Post.

In the early 1960s, a new Jewish school was established in Wuzaba, near Ambober. It made sense to have the
educational facilities closer to the major Jewish population
center in Gondar. The Asmara school, which was far away,
was eventually closed; Noah, who had become director of
that school, moved to Gondar.

Some six years or more after they had gone to Israel to
study, the majority of youngsters from Kfar Batya returned
to Ethiopia. Shortly after their return, they paid a formal
visit to Haile Selassie with Noah. The emperor said to
them, "It is good that you have come. I think that if you go
to work on government projects now, you will help your people and Ethiopia at the same time."

But they rejected his offer. "The education we have is
a Jewish education," they told him. "We were meant to help
our people." And they went to the school at Wuzaba to teach.

Some years later, the school at Wuzaba burned – there
seems no doubt that the fire was set deliberately. The building itself, along with all the books, was destroyed. The
school was closed. During this period, financial support
from the Jewish world stopped for the teachers from Wuzaba. They suffered a great deal – they had no money and it
seemed that no one cared about them. Two went back to Addis Ababa; others found work with the government.

Those who were sincere stayed, and suffered, with
their own people. These are the ones who have only recently
arrived in Israel; they were in prison for a year and a half,
charged as Zionist agents. Ultimately, it was because of
them that I decided to leave Addis Ababa and go help.

A few years after the school at Wuzaba was burned, a
new school was opened at Ambober, and another in Teda.
The Kfar Batya teachers who remained went to one or the

other of these. However, there was not enough money to run the schools properly. Ambober had additional difficulties because of government interference; some of the teachers sent there served as spies.

After the revolution in 1974, an international Jewish philanthropic organization, the Jewish Organization for Service, began operations in Ethiopia. JOS took over the whole educational structure that until then had been supervised by Noah.

Although Noah was financed to some degree by the Department of Diaspora Jewry of the Jewish Agency, by caring private individuals from the U.S., Canada, and Holland, and by a British organization called the Falasha Welfare Association, he still did not have sufficient funds and was forced to concentrate in places like Ambober, while outlying Jewish villages remained neglected.

JOS changed that. Their prime mover was a British philanthropist named Saul Kaye who had been affiliated with the Falasha Welfare Association. He and others had visited Gondar, and had become convinced that the superior resources of JOS would improve the situation substantially.

The man hired to head JOS operations was Shimon Yerushalami, an Israeli who had been in Ethiopia for many years. Yerushalami decided to give the number-two position to Walbeyu Kabeda, a non-Jewish Ethiopian who had worked with him in an Israeli firm formerly located in Ethiopia.

The remaining Kfar Batya teachers—about six at that point—were upset about the appointment of Kabeda, a non-Jew, as a JOS administrator. Yerushalami assured them that Kabeda would work only as an accountant in the Addis offices and would have no professional contact with the teachers in the field.

But then, Yerushalami was suddenly dismissed by

JOS, and a fellow from Switzerland, Jacob Goldvasser, was brought in as the new program head. Goldvasser put Noah on a pension. This meant that for all practical purposes, he was barred from active participation. Following Yerushalami's lead, he named Kabeda chief administrator of JOS in Ethiopia. From the offices in Addis, they began operating, despite the opposition of every Jew in JOS to having a non-Jew administer a Jewish organization. Goldvasser's goal was to preserve JOS; he was afraid that he would be accused of being a Zionist discriminator by the Ethiopian government. But, at the time, it was often hard for us to understand his behavior.

An Israeli, Michael Rosen, was hired as project director in the field in Gondar. Even when battling a tense political situation in the north, he was a highly competent man who managed to create dynamic programs. Rosen was strongly opposed to having a non-Jew as administrator. He knew that although Kabeda himself was not a professional, he would bring others who were. And that is exactly what happened. Kabeda brought his people, non-Jews, into the program as administrators, becoming very powerful in the process.

The JOS officials outside the country were operating with good intentions, but they didn't realize what the result of their policies would be. They had determined that JOS would function more effectively in Ethiopia as a nonsectarian program, and they felt that, in order to show the government their sincerity, they had to employ a non-Jew in a key position. They assumed he would follow orders.

But Kabeda had other ideas. The JOS officials had no knowledge of who the educated Ethiopian Jews were or where they might be found. Educated Jews could easily have been trained to fill every one of the administrative positions. Yet Kabeda had led them to believe that there were no Jewish administrators available and that, therefore, non-Jews had to be employed to fill the key positions.

Kabeda hired a man named Aletaw Dessie to work as Gondar administrator. Aletaw, however, had ties to the antigovernment Ethiopian People's Revolutionary Party (EPRP). Threatened with exposure, he ran. Rosen then brought in Takele Achenafi, a well-respected Ethiopian Jew with excellent credentials, to be administrator in Gondar.

When Jacob Goldvasser was moved to JOS's international headquarters in Brussels, a French Jew, Daniel Mendes, was brought in to take his place in Addis. Mendes was a good man but, like Goldvasser before him, he was worried about protecting JOS. He left Kabeda in place.

There were some dire results. First, Kabeda had his department heads identify all the Jews who worked under them. Then Achenafi was sabotaged.

Kabeda came to Gondar once a month. He had a friendly relationship with Public Security there and even with Major Melaku, my childhood enemy, who was now the provincial administrator of Gondar. With the connivance of Security personnel, it seems that Kabeda arranged to have Takele charged as antirevolutionary and arrested. The charge was patently false; Takele was not involved in politics at all.

Rosen complained to authorities about this arrest, and was promised that Takele would be let out of prison the following Saturday. Then, on the Thursday before Takele was to have been released, Kabeda returned to Gondar—but instead of going to the JOS offices, he went to a hotel, spent time with Public Security people and returned to Addis.

Takele was not released. On that Shabbat, the day he was supposed to have been freed, word reached us that he had been murdered in prison.

Rosen was a man of feeling; having no stomach to

continue his work, he went to Addis Ababa. From there, with an assist from Kabeda and his associates, he was pushed out of the organization.

The murder of Takele took place after I had been released from prison in early 1979. When I heard about it, I realized how fortunate I was: I could have been Takele.

5

The Destruction

Late in 1979, I was asked to work for JOS. Takele was dead and Rosen had been let go. Because of all the political turmoil at this time, Jacob Goldvasser had come back from Brussels. Then four Jewish teachers originally from Kfar Batya had been charged with antigovernment activity and arrested.

Goldvasser, Mendes, and Kabeda invited me to a meeting at which they made an offer. I accepted because I was very angry—because of Kabeda, and because our innocent brother had been killed. Then I heard that Jewish teachers, also innocent, were being jailed. I intended to help these teachers and then to return to Addis, so I signed a one-year contract to direct the Jewish educational system in Ethiopia, working from Gondar; I wound up staying almost two years.

Not long after our meeting, Goldvasser was fired for political reasons that may have included complaints Noah registered against him. The man who took over his responsibilities, Benjamin Milbauer, came into Gondar to assess the JOS program there. He made his position quite clear: the JOS program was a development program, not a political program. Milbauer seemed reasonable, sophisticated, and good-hearted; I loved him. He was so deeply Jewish in his attitudes, and so sensitive to our issues, that he motivated me to try my best.

When I went into Gondar to start working, Kabeda was there. I was friendly to him, just as I was friendly to everyone—the Security people and even Melaku, who had been my classmate years before. I knew that I would have to be on good terms with him; he was a big man now. The head of Security had known me at the university, when he had studied psychology for his police work. He became a good friend, although he had little awareness of the Jews because he was not originally from Gondar.

Carefully, deliberately, I began to spend time with these people who were in positions of power in Gondar—all people who drank a great deal. My Jewish friends were confused by my behavior, but I knew exactly what I was doing. My first order of business was to find out what the charges against the Jewish teachers were.

The Kfar Batya teachers, and Rosen, when he was still with JOS, had pushed to move the main JOS Ethiopian headquarters to Gondar, where the Jews actually lived. But the important men in Addis wanted to stay where they were. Kabeda certainly did not want to live among Jews. The excuse given for staying in Addis was that it was an international city, where communication was better. However, the group of teachers pressing for the move was strong, and Kabeda found it necessary to undermine them.

One of the Kfar Batya teachers had been responsible for distributing money to Jews whose property had been destroyed by antirevolutionaries, and JOS had given him a large sum of cash for this purpose.

There was a non-Jew who had been brought from Addis to work as a storekeeper, that is, supervise the JOS warehouse in Gondar. It was clearly ridiculous to bring a man such a distance for this purpose when so many local people were available; what is more, the man was paid a huge salary. The storekeeper was suspected of antirevolutionary activities and arrested. Maybe they suspected him because he carried around a lot of money and went drinking in places where antirevolutionaries were seen. Or, maybe, as the Jewish people of Gondar believed, he had been brought in from Addis in the first place in order to be used and it was all planned.

When he was put in jail, he started naming people who were supposedly antirevolutionaries. Among those he named were the Kfar Batya teachers. The Security people went after them; they found the money earmarked for distribution in the home of the teacher responsible for it. He was charged with using it for antirevolutionary purposes. When the teacher tried to explain what the money was for, they didn't believe him. "You are a Zionist agent," they told him, and they tortured him brutally.

Having discovered all of this, I suspected that the non-Jews working inside the JOS program had pushed these Jews out using JOS money to bribe the Security people. Out of my own money, I bought the Security people. It was very expensive, but I had no choice. I poured good whiskey for them, and not only absorbed all the information they fed me, but also gained influence with them. After seven months, three of the four teachers were released. In another three months, the last one was let go. They came out of prison crippled, but they were free.

As I watched what was going on, it became clear that graft was one of the main reasons Kabeda was trying to get all Jews of authority out of JOS. I saw it with my own eyes. He was building a villa outside Addis, in Bolle, near the international airport. JOS had a truck, used to take building materials for school construction and so forth from a main warehouse in Addis to the Gondar area, which was then supposed to return to Addis empty. The driver, however, was returning from Gondar with material for Kabeda still in his truck. Those Jews who knew about this, like the new storekeeper in Gondar, were not in a position to interfere.

One day I caught Kabeda at it. There was a large amount of concrete, iron for building reinforcement, and water pipes—all very expensive items. They had been signed for as if they were going to go out to the project area of Ambober. The heads of each of the departments involved—the water department, the construction department, and so forth—had cooperated in the deception. The overall approval had come from a man named Major Tesfa.

Major Tesfa was a close associate of Major Melaku's. Kabeda had brought him into JOS's Gondar offices to serve as administrator in place of the murdered Takele. Tesfa did nothing but sit in his office lending the authority of his presence. His approval was considered the equal of Melaku's, and he was willing to approve whatever Kabeda wanted.

Until then, I'd been friendly with everyone; I was no threat. Now I traced the distribution of this material. I went to the new storekeeper in Gondar, a man named Sahalu. I visited him quietly, at night. He was frightened, but confirmed that the materials were not being used in Ambober. I felt that I had Kabeda; I immediately called Mendes and told him.

"You're a liar!" he said. "I don't believe you." An honest response would have been different—"Really? Are you sure?" Mendes didn't want to deal with it; he wasn't strong enough to take on Kabeda. He chose to keep quiet instead.

That was my turning point—I changed totally. Instead of being cordial to everyone, I adopted an official line: this material belongs to the Jewish people. No more, I said, will the rich milk JOS for their own purposes. I told Sahalu, the storekeeper, that I didn't want this to happen anymore. I asked him to sign receipts for material, and I photocopied everything.

A month later, Mendes came to Gondar. He was not a stupid man. "Mendes," I told him. "You choose, or you lose. If you don't get back the material that belongs to JOS, I will leave."

When I worked to get the Jewish teachers out of prison, I wasn't looking for credit from Mendes. But he knew what I had accomplished and what my value to the organization was at the time. I left him no choice. He took severe measures, calling each of the department heads who had signed for Kabeda's materials, and Major Tesfa. "Return it," he told them, "or pay in cash. If you don't I will close the project down and we'll all go home."

Kabeda paid in cash. Secretly, Mendes admitted to me that I was responsible, but he also wasn't careful about protecting me. Once Kabeda had paid, there were repercussions.

Mendes hadn't told Kabeda that he'd gotten his information from me. He claimed to have gone into the field himself and checked. But Kabeda wondered what had made Mendes check at that point, so many months after the fact. He wanted to know who'd told Mendes.

Kabeda knew that the storekeeper was a fearful man and that the cashier, an Ethiopian Jewish woman named Yeshwork, was also afraid. He felt sure that neither was responsible for telling on him, nor Yakov Getu, a quiet department head, for that matter. So, then, who? "The new man. He smiles all the time. But what is he thinking?" Kabeda and his friends decided that I was dangerous, and it was true. After Mendes went back to Addis, Kabeda left a note saying that he and his Christian brothers in JOS would get me.

While in Gondar, I lived in the JOS office building. Tensions were high, so I had not brought my family; they remained back in Addis. Most of the time I was in the field;

I didn't like sitting behind a desk, it was important to me to be out with the people. It was my habit to go to a hotel in the morning, have a cup of coffee and a cigarette, and then go into the field. I had a driver who took me in a JOS car.

One day I returned from the field, from Wogerra. My driver dropped me at a hotel to get something to eat. He took the car to the compound next to the JOS building for the night. There were two guards there, one Jewish and one not. I ate, and came back to the JOS office building. It was 8:30 p.m. There were two men waiting outside. I thought it was unusual that they should still be there at that hour; most of the workers took off even before the work day was finished.

"Good evening," I said, and passed by them. They were careful not to appear suspicious in front of the Jewish guard. I went into the building and entered my living quarters. It was a hot night and I left my door open behind me. I did not know that the two men had followed me into the building. They had given the guard the impression that they had either been invited, or were to have a meeting with me. I was taking off my jacket in my warm room when I heard something. I turned towards the door and saw one of them entering the room.

I could not see the second man. He remained outside the door.

The other one came at me. He had a big gold ring on his finger and hit me across the nose so that it caught me. I let out a shout and reached forward to grab him by his hair. I held tight, his face was brought close to mine. I was bleeding, and the blood was running down my nose and into my mouth. I spit that blood into his face and kept shouting at him. He was stronger than I, but I jabbed at his groin and then reached for a bottle of mineral water to hit him with; in that moment I suddenly felt weak. He broke loose and ran away.

When he ran out of the building, the Jewish guard saw him and hit him with a long stick, in Ethiopian style. The man disappeared. The guard came back to me and saw my condition, but I told him, "Keep quiet, or it will be dangerous for JOS."

The bleeding stopped and I slept for a while, just as I was. Then I went in an ambulance to the hospital to be treated, and the guard called the police. The man was arrested and held for the night.

I thought at first that they had intended to kill me, but later, as I looked back on what had happened, I realized that they simply wanted to frighten me into leaving.

Before too long, most of the Jews in the area were aware of what had happened. I didn't say anything, but my face was swollen for a week. When Jewish teachers came to my office to speak with me, the guard took them aside and told them. In no time, the whole community knew.

"Ah, this is the second time," they said. "Once before an educated Jewish son came to help us, and they killed him. Now they want to kill this one too. Before they will kill him, we will kill them."

It was satisfying to be able to organize the people of the area, so that they would start to think on their own behalf as Jews. Others had controlled them until then. Now a pin could not be moved without my knowing about it. From every corner information came directly into my office. The sabotage of JOS stopped.

Before the harassment took place, members of the local Jewish community simply had not believed that I had come from Addis to help them. Once, a Jewish storekeeper in Teda had done a careless job and I had criticized him and then written him a warning letter. However, for the protection of the Jews, such letters were kept from Kabeda, who would have used them for unconscionable purposes. I considered such matters to be internal Ethiopian Jewish affairs.

The next time I returned to Teda, I was met by the angry storekeeper, who recited an Amharic expression that literally means, "When a woman is poor, everyone comes from above to stretch her genitals. When a woman is rich, it can't be done to her anymore."

This man didn't know me; he wanted me to hear his complaints and improve his difficult situation. Even so, when he said that to me, I cried and tried to explain to him that I was not there to use him. After the attack, when I saw him again, he said that he regretted what he had said.

Finding friends was wonderful: Yakov Getu, who was shy; the gentle storekeeper Sahalu; Yeshwork, the cashier, and others. They were all good people who came to work with me. Yeshwork had problems because she was in a society that sees women as weaker, and so there was a time when she allowed herself to be manipulated. When she came to understand how she could help her people by passing information, she cooperated. There were similar interactions with others; our unity was sincere and affectionate.

Every month, Mendes came from Addis for a few days. And whenever the Jews came to him with information, he acted quickly to stop abuses. He was marvelous in those days. The only problem was that sometimes the Jews were afraid to tell him what they knew, thinking it might get back to Kabeda, so he wasn't always as well informed as he might have been. As the unity of the Jews in JOS became greater, a new problem was created: JOS employees were divided into two camps—Jews and non-Jews, each caring only about their own.

Even in such things as salaries, the non-Jews were

favored. I knew of one Jew with university qualifications who was paid 1,100 birr per month for a position of responsibility, and I knew of a non-Jew, who was only a high school graduate from Dessei, without certification, who worked as a technician and received 1,200 birr.

The frustration was enormous. Non-Jews flaunted their higher earnings. Top JOS officials permitted this inequity because they felt that Jews were working for their people, and not for money: if the Jews of the world were contributing money for this program, then the Jewish workers had to contribute by accepting smaller salaries. There may have been a valid principle here—one that I can understand and even agree with—but dissension was created because it was never explained properly to the Jews.

The friction grew worse day by day and political suspicions and charges emerged. The non-Jews used the politics of the government to attack us. Lies were told, hints of dishonesty were leaked. I began to realize that people in the government whom I had been careful to cultivate before weren't seeing me as a friend any more.

I had some responsibilities with the Ministry of Education in the province. An Anti-Illiteracy Campaign had been organized within the Ministry and I was participating as the JOS delegate. Suddenly, I was kicked out. I knew I was now considered suspect.

I stayed close to Security people in order to acquire information, although I never used it in any way except to protect myself and the other Jews. Although I didn't care for his Communist ideology, the head of Security was a good man. He thought I was a Communist, and for a long time he did not know I was Jewish. When he finally realized that I was, he told me Major Melaku was anti-Jewish. He said Melaku was a stupid drunkard and a Hitlerish type who had killed many innocent youngsters, and that he was not a Communist. I believed all of these things because I had known Melaku from the beginning. Whatever Melaku said during the day, I knew by that evening; the security man was protecting me.

The first accusations that I was a Zionist agent came not from Major Melaku, but from the non-Jews in JOS. The anti-Jewish atmosphere was very difficult for me to handle with a cool head. JOS was divided into departments, for education and administration, but only two of the responsible men within these departments were Ethiopian Jews—my friend Yakov Getu and myself. The others were non-Jews.

When I arrived in 1979, there were twelve elementary schools within the educational system, with 1,012 students attending. By the time I left there were 5,202 students in total, and twenty-two elementary schools in twenty villages. We had opened a high school in Ambober and we had four training schools at the high school level, in Wolleka and Teda. In Wolleka, there was woodworking and pottery and, for the girls, sewing and decoration. In Teda, there was a metalwork program. We deliberately did not bring sophisticated machinery in for the woodworking; the idea was to train the students for cottage industries first, using what would be available to them in the villages. Another training program for women was being planned, but acute tensions made it impossible. I recruited teachers for these enlarged programs, especially at the lower levels, by taking high school graduates from secular schools and sending them to college for education courses.

These programs were being enlarged while I was being harassed by the Security people. They said that my training programs were not nonsectarian. "You are only for the Falashas," they charged. (The academic program was also supposed to be nonsectarian, but there was less concern about it. The practical training courses had the added incentive of providing pocket money for those students who attended. These courses interested the non-Jews.)

There happened to be a tribe in the Gondar area called the Kimants — an oppressed minority. So in an effort to avoid tensions with the authorities, I placed two Kimants for every thirteen Jews in each class.

My efforts were not considered enough. I was told I had to balance the students half and half. This would have meant a bigger expense to the program than I could afford. Pressure to do this came from within JOS, from the non-Jews. But Mendes, as the program's director, supported me in my decision not to enroll such a high percentage of non-Jews. And that decision was finally accepted by the Security forces.

I had not hired the teachers in the vocational training programs. Most of them had been recruited to Gondar from Addis Ababa by Kabeda.

I had found no organization within the academic programs of JOS. No attempt was made to control the students, who came and went as they pleased. Teaching was done by trial and error, without planned lessons. Most teachers had never been given any guidance on how to present material successfully. But even so, many were competent and serious instructors such as the non-Jewish pottery and handcrafts teachers. A French Jew, named Emmanuel, who taught metalwork, was also excellent. One woman who was a close friend of Melaku's was hired to teach sewing, at a sky-high salary, but she had no idea about what she was doing.

For my first seven months I had made no changes; I had simply moved about in the field getting to better understand the situation. I sat in on classes, observing the quality of the teaching, and also taking note of which teachers were Jewish and which were not.

Then I decided which teachers to keep, preparing

lessons plans for each of them. I visited every classroom, taught demonstration lessons, and supervised.

In total, I was working with roughly seventy-five teachers. At the elementary level, almost all of the secular teachers were Jewish; at the junior-high level, about 80 percent were. But by the senior-high level, almost none were Jewish. Those Jewish teachers who were available at the higher levels worked for the government. It was extremely hard to get them to come back to the Jewish villages—they were afraid that if they took jobs with JOS, they would never be able to get another government job. So all the university graduates I had working as teachers were non-Jews.

I made a special effort to motivate the Jewish teachers and to direct them so that they had a feeling for why they were there. It seemed to me that the competency of the Jewish teachers was low compared to that of the government teachers.

In order to improve their academic levels, I selected five villages as centers. Teachers in these villages went to a nearby secular high school and JOS agreed to absorb the expense. These teachers continued to teach during the day and attended courses at night. Those who completed this program were then required to go to remote villages and relieve teachers there, so that others in turn could benefit from the same program. What I did not have access to were pedagogic training centers; the government had these. I worked out an agreement with the Ministry of Education to take four teachers to participate in the summer educational seminars. The expense of this was also absorbed by JOS.

The Kfar Batya teachers served as religious and Hebrew teachers within this system, as well as teachers of arts and crafts and agriculture. The religious classes were combined with secular classes during the day. For example, there might have been math, science, Amharic, health, Hebrew, and Jewish values. Hebrew was always taught by a Kfar Batya graduate, Jewish values sometimes by a *kes* who had graduated from the Asmara program.

A couple of years later, when JOS was gone from Ethiopia, it was the Kfar Batya graduates who suffered the most. Their skill was teaching Hebrew, their association was with Israel; they were without secular academic skills that were recognized by the Ethiopian government.

The beginning of the end was near. As tensions between the Jews and the non-Jews increased, the atmosphere was charged with suspicion; new false charges were made daily.

Within the organization the Jews protected each other. I also tried to be careful by never speaking about the government, Major Melaku, or Public Security in a negative way. I pretended to sympathize with all of it. However, the more intelligent people in the government sector did not believe me, because what I was doing and what I was saying were clearly two different things.

For a long time I could not be touched because of my friendship with the captain in Public Security. When I finally was defeated, it was in part because of a break between this man and Major Melaku. The non-Jews of JOS got to Melaku and let him know the captain was my friend and, therefore, a JOS sympathizer. They had reached Melaku through Melaku's friend, Major Tesfa, who sat in the offices of JOS. Tesfa was a fairly harmless man who was paid a huge salary to sit and drink and do nothing. He was quite happy in his role, but others told him he was powerless because of me and ultimately he went to Melaku. Melaku had the captain in Security recalled from Gondar and sent to another province.

I was shocked, but I was still in control. All they could do was continue to harass me in the hope that I would go. They wanted JOS to be their fat cow giving milk all of the time.

The new man who came in to replace my friend as head of Public Security pleased the non-Jews; they saw his appointment as an opportunity to defeat me. He began to call me every so often, to accuse me of being a Zionist agent and of working for the CIA.

Of course, I was a Zionist.

I felt very strongly about the existence, protection, and development of Jerusalem—of Zion. But that is not what they meant. To call someone a Zionist was to say that he was a racist and opposed to the struggle of the oppressed masses in the Middle East—the same nonsense as in the Soviet Union. Because of the way I shaped JOS's educational system, I was suspect. They felt I had betrayed the government that educated me by working for an organization that had not invested a penny to make me what I was. It was as if I were a traitor, loyal to non-Ethiopian forces. What intensified this was that Jews were beginning to escape from Ethiopia, and JOS was suspected of being involved in this secret exodus. They saw me as the person in JOS who was likely to have been organizing this. As far as the CIA was concerned, there was no reason to even think that I had anything to do with them. Charges that I did were simply lies, made to weaken my position.

My ability to continue to have good sources of information rapidly became a matter of life and death. My opponents were people capable of murder—I had to protect myself. It was forbidden to carry arms into the field, but after the incident of harassment I did keep a long knife concealed in my house. I was determined to go down fighting if I were to be attacked again.

JOS had six drivers, only one of whom was a Jew. A rather foolish man, he was the secretary for a socialist workers' association that functioned within the framework of JOS. When I went with these drivers into the field, I always felt uneasy, wondering if what I said would be reported back to the Public Security office. I did not even feel comfortable with the Jewish driver, whose name was Derso, because of his connection to the workers' association. In order to be careful about what I revealed, I developed a way of communicating with Jews in the field based on body language rather than speech. The people there knew what was going on and spoke to me differently when we were alone.

As far as the workers' association itself was concerned, there were times when I thought what they did was right. They fought corruption. They were angry about the inequity of salaries between the non-Jews and Jews and complained to the JOS director about it.

But there were other things they did that were simply ridiculous and in one case rather funny. I was part of a labor-negotiating team that met within the framework of the association. On one side were the workers, all Jewish, representing their interests. On the other side were those representing the employer, JOS: the lawyer for JOS, Major Tesfa, and myself. We were supposed to negotiate salary and benefits according to government guidelines. I found myself somewhere in the middle of this collective bargaining. The lawyer and Tesfa were against everything the workers requested; the workers were against the employer's position.

Then the workers made a proposal that brought everyone together. The secretary of the socialist group suggested that if JOS left Ethiopia, whether freely or not, the workers should be paid seven years' salary as compensation. This suggestion was unanimously accepted, despite the fact that it went against all the government guidelines.

Moreover, both the JOS lawyer and Major Tesfa decided to reclassify themselves as workers. I laughed and told the lawyer what I thought of him. Later, the workers told me that they had brought that proposal deliberately to reveal his and Tesfa's true colors. Of course, the director of JOS did not accept the proposal.

However, it was not funny when the frustrated association began to attack JOS as a Zionist organization. This happened, in part, because of the spread of Communist ideology in Ethiopia at this time.

Every week, a discussion forum, conducted by the workers, was held for two hours. Attendance was compulsory for all Ethiopians, whether workers or management. I went as an employer's representative though I hated to do so, and hated the philosophy on which the meetings were based. I had to go or I would be accused of being an anti-Communist. I knew that I was already suspect, but that there was no tangible evidence yet.

Evidence was crucial.

Before I had come to Gondar, Major Melaku, who ran the province, had ordered mass arrests and executed numerous political opponents. Much of what he had done was aimed at the Jews. The central government, assuming that Melaku was a loyal Communist, had given him license to carry on. They saw things in terms of a class struggle and assumed that if Melaku arrested someone, it was because the person was an antirevolutionary. But when an outcry about Melaku's behavior finally reached the central government, he was warned: before you arrest someone, you'd better have evidence. Evidence gathered before the arrest was best, but in any case, evidence would have to be presented to a committee that sat in Addis within twenty-four hours after an arrest.

There was a time when it had suited Melaku's purposes to be in favor of JOS. I had attended a meeting once and heard him talk about how the whole Ethiopian nation was benefiting from the JOS construction done in Ethiopia. "JOS has built a marvelous road, with large sums of money," he said. "If JOS leaves Ethiopia tomorrow, do you think they will roll up the road and take it back with them? Will they take the school buildings? These are the true gifts of JOS to the Ethiopian people."

But time and politics had changed things. Little by little, Melaku had become more negative towards JOS because of the information he was receiving from the non-Jewish workers. Now, working with JOS too closely in a Jewish fashion was interpreted as being anti-Communist. Eventually, Melaku came to the position that JOS had to be thrown out of Ethiopia.

I was being watched for my loyalties. I had developed a syllabus that included Jewish education. Several times I was called into the offices of the Ministry of Education and told to follow the Ministry curriculum and syllabus only, not my amended version. Their curriculum emphasized Communism; Jewish education was no longer considered acceptable. The government agents in the province were becoming blatantly anti-Semitic.

On one occasion a large group of Jews trying to leave the country was apprehended in Gondar and jailed. There were about ninety of them; one was a JOS worker—a mechanic—and this increased suspicion that JOS was officially involved in the escapes.

One of the things the Security office did to gather information about whether JOS was involved in secret emigration was to hire a disgruntled Jew who had previously been a JOS technican. His assignment was to come to the head office in Gondar, poke around and chat, and then carry information back to Public Security. But I was aware of what he was doing. In fact, I secured some very interesting information from this man and fed him information about myself—about my "Communist" loyalties—which he then carried back.

The non-Jewish teachers in the vocational training programs continued to present a problem for me. The woodworking teacher, a lazy, drinking man, was unhappy because his department did not have the kind of sophisticated machinery he was used to. He was born and brought up in the area that Melaku had come from and he was proud of that. He claimed to be a Communist; although I had the feeling he didn't really know anything, he was chairman of the discussion forum of the workers' association. Through his work on this committee, he had a link to Melaku. I tried to motivate him to teach well, but I found it very difficult. He had skills and contacts that actually made me afraid of him. When he wanted to fix a charge on someone, he could do a very good job of it.

The woman who was supposed to teach sewing also presented a serious problem. She did not know her material, and before long her students were complaining about her. I went to supervise her regularly and saw how poorly she did. I brought Tesfa with me so that he would report back to Kabeda. After three warnings, I decided to fire her. It was very difficult—her boyfriend was Melaku's second in command. I informed the director of my decision, and he told the JOS lawyer. Now, suddenly, all the non-Jews in administrative positions in JOS, pretending to be concerned employers, became involved: the lawyer, Major Tesfa, Kabeda, and department heads. And she was still in the classroom.

The students were frustrated and began to cause disruptions in the classroom. The teacher complained to Major Tesfa, accusing me of being responsible. Before I knew what had happened, Major Tesfa had secretly written a letter to a police investigating committee, and they arrested all the girls in the class. Then I became exceedingly angry.

The charge against them was that, wishing to leave the country themselves, they were boycotting classes in sympathy with Jews in prison for trying to escape. It was a serious accusation.

I went to the prison and offered myself as a guarantor for them. There I was told, in front of the students, that I could not be a guarantor because I was a suspected Zionist agent and a member of the CIA. I was shocked. This was the first time I had been openly labeled.

Major Tesfa claimed to know nothing about what was going on, but I had a photocopy of the letter he had written the police. I called the director and spoke to him at great length.

By the next day, most of the girls were released. Four of them, however, were kept as ringleaders suspected of cooperating with me. For a couple of weeks, those students and I suffered a great deal. Major Tesfa was keeping those girls in prison as a weapon against me.

Mendes made the trip to Gondar. It all weighed heavily on me, and I told him I would not forget the betrayal. "You are here to help the Jewish people, but they collect their fat salaries in order to destroy us. I don't care about the organization any more. We are not politicians," I said. "We should not be involved in the country's politics. We're concerned with other, important things. Isn't it our goal to teach Jewish values? Isn't this our whole purpose?"

After that, Mendes no longer wanted to see me, but he knew very clearly what I was talking about. The girls were released. Mendes arranged it by leaning on Major Tesfa; Tesfa was afraid of him.

Now I felt absolutely driven. I knew that my time was

limited, that if I didn't accomplish things then, I never would. I was determined to give it my best. I didn't sleep; I was crazy.

During these last days, I became very emotional and suspicious. I didn't even visit my mother. I knew I would be followed if I did and that if I spoke to my relatives, and were to try to escape later, they would be questioned and tortured.

The attacks against me had become so sophisticated that I was never sure what would come next. The vocational training semester was over and we had to budget new programs. As before, I assigned two Kimants to thirteen Jews. Suddenly Public Security called me in. I didn't know how they knew what I was doing, but they were getting their information from the inside. The head of Security told me I was discriminating.

"The government of Ethiopia educated you, not the government of Israel," he said. "You were supposed to be here for one year. It's time for you to leave ... otherwise ... "

I refused to resign. "I'll die here," I said.

"Who will kill you?" he asked. "You'll kill yourself, no one else will."

When I returned to the head offices, none of my friends was around. I quietly made my way to Major Tesfa's office; there I overheard him talking with the non-Jewish administrators. "I made it, I made it," he was saying. "Now it's his problem—he'll face it." There was loud laughter and shouting.

I went back to my office and sat down to do my job as I always did. I knew they couldn't kill me—they still did not have tangible evidence—and I still had my contacts with the political organizers of the Communist Party and Public Security. I would still have time before I would have to flee.

Kabeda and Mendes came to Gondar for a labor negotiation held in the main offices of JOS. The evening before the negotiations began, Kabeda made the rounds, visiting my friends, trying to turn them against me. To Yakov he said, "These idiot Falashas! I wanted to help them, but they don't want to be helped!" To another, he said, "It's Shmuel's fault they don't understand me." The plan had been to pressure me, but after this slander was repeated to me the next morning, I was angered even further and determined to firmly stand my ground.

That morning I attended the negotiation meeting with Major Tesfa, and the JOS lawyer, who turned it against the workers' interests. Derso, the secretary of the workers' association, was disgusted. He turned to Kabeda and said, "You bribe everybody, that's why we can't win."

As everyone was leaving, I overheard Kabeda say to Tesfa, "Punish him and show me just how tough you are."

Most of the people went out into the field for the day, but Tesfa and I returned to our offices. Derso, too, had stayed behind to ask the payroll office for an advance. From my office, I heard Major Tesfa call to Derso.

The young man went into Tesfa's office and the door was closed. I began hearing shouts for help and I ran into the hall. I called Derso from outside the office and then tried to break the door down. Major Tesfa opened it; he was quivering because he had been caught. He had been hitting Derso brutally.

"Are you mad?" I asked. "What kind of a person are you? Isn't he a human being? To punish him, you will kill him? You're just an ignorant bull. I overheard everything Kabeda said to you this morning."

Derso ran out, and I went back to my office, but I could not work. I was agitated all day. At the end of the day, I saw Kabeda coming up the stairs and I began to shake. I wanted to tear him to pieces. The metalwork teacher, Emmanuel, came into the building with his wife. They saw the emotional state I was in and tried to calm me down.

But when I went outside, I saw Kabeda, this time walking with Mendes, and became agitated again. "You idiot!" I screamed at Kabeda. "What kind of trouble are you trying to make?"

"Are you mad?" he asked me.

"Yes," I said. "You are making me mad."

The three of us went into an office and closed the door. Kabeda made his charge: "You're always on the Falashas' side."

"Do you think I'm a fool?" I asked. "I know what you're doing. I am here to protect my people. It isn't enough that you don't distribute money fairly. It isn't enough that you put your people into positions of power. Now you terrorize people using Melaku's methods. No more. You can't do it anymore!"

"Are you mad, Shmuel?" said Mendes. "What are you saying?"

"Shut up," I said to him. "Shut up. If you don't know what your people are doing, then just keep quiet and learn."

Sometimes Mendes was on my side. There had been times when he controlled things so well that the others thought of him as a bone in their throats. But when tension was high, and he got nervous, he looked on me as radical, extreme. And he was right.

That night I was so disturbed that I put everything aside and just slept. It was good that I did. The next morning, I went to my office and worked, feeling refreshed. Mendes was taken aside by the French couple, Emmanuel and his wife. They spoke to him out of a common bond of French culture and tried to convince him I was being fair.

What was wrong, they said, was that I had gotten so emotionally involved in the situation.

Mendes now wanted to talk to me, but I refused to have anything to do with him. What I did do was approach Kabeda and charge him. "What were you saying to my friends about me?" I asked him. "You think I don't know what's going on? Nothing is secret."

Kabeda, perhaps uncomfortable with what I'd said to him, then convinced Mendes that it was important to prove that I was a liar. They called a meeting of the Ethiopian Jewish workers.

That day I went out into the field. I returned at six in the evening, knowing nothing about the meeting. The Jews had all been told except me. I closed up my office, and went over to my friend Yakov's office, hoping to spend the evening with him.

Then everyone started gathering there, even Tesfa. Mendes turned to me and said, "Don't disturb me the way you did last night. We're going to have a short conference."

"Okay," I said. I immediately understood that they had planned to defeat me, but I didn't intend to let it happen. Kabeda had come assuming he could terrorize the Jews as he had done in the past.

"I won't disturb you," I told Mendes. "Yesterday I was very emotional, because I was forced to swallow too much. I had seen Tesfa strike Derso that morning. He is Jewish and I thought he had been hit for that reason. Perhaps I misunderstood what I saw, but I was there and you weren't. Today, I've spoken about it and I'm all right. I won't disturb you, so long as you run a democratic meeting."

Kabeda began with his own defense, but was quickly silenced.

My friends spoke, starting with Yakov. "Yes," he said to

Kabeda, "in my house you said things about Shmuel. I kept quiet because you were my guest, but I did not sleep that night. Every time you come to Gondar, you cause agitation and trouble."

Yeshwork reminded Kabeda he had told her that when money was misallocated she should not tell Mendes. "And you told me that Shmuel's arrival here changed me."

Others spoke as well. Mendes understood it all.

Then it was my turn. "I know that the JOS program is a good one," I said. "But there is a stinking JOS administration here in Gondar. It's as if JOS is a net and the Jewish workers are caught in that net, trapped, in order to be killed. Politics are being used against us. I am an Ethiopian, not an Israeli, but I am also a Jew. Because I'm Jewish, I'm called antirevolutionary and because Kabeda is not, he's praised as a Communist.

"If you want to work with us, don't accuse us, and don't persecute us," I said to Kabeda. "Don't evaluate our culture. Who are you to judge? Until now I have never been defeated as a Jew. But here in a Jewish program, we are suddenly all in danger, and you are responsible."

I knew Kabeda was a dangerous man, and that I'd have to prepare for the revenge he'd take. But I'd wanted to reach Daniel Mendes.

What Kabeda did was really very foolish; he didn't understand the consequences of his action. He thought he could eliminate me by convincing Melaku that JOS was bad. He didn't realize that in the process he would also eliminate JOS.

Melaku was an alcoholic, and Kabeda was adept at creating the right atmosphere so Melaku would believe him. They met outside Addis Ababa, in Kazanchizin. Kabeda told Melaku that I was a Zionist, a dangerous man responsible for helping people escape across the Ethiopian border. He also accused me of discriminating against Ethiopians, and maintained that everyone was infected since I'd come into the JOS program.

There was some truth to what he said. Before my arrival, the Jews had tended to fight among themselves, which had suited everyone else very well. My coming had brought a kind of unity, and that made me dangerous. Harassment had not succeeded in forcing me out. Finally, arranging to have me put in prison seemed the most sensible way to get rid of me.

I had taught myself to be keenly sensitive to my environment, which made it more difficult to bring charges against me. My problem was that I was emotional. Sometimes I was unhappy with myself about this. I would have liked to have always responded reasonably, but sometimes I tried to be heroic. I might have been better off if I'd been more passive.

Major Tesfa and the others seemed very happy; something was probably being planned. I waited for a call from Security. On a Monday evening, Major Melaku came back to Gondar, and all the workers were called for a meeting in his office.

The meeting was held on a Tuesday, at noon. There were some government officials present, and Melaku was protected by his bodyguards. When he got up to speak, we could see he'd been drinking.

Nothing surprised me. Melaku announced that he had the power to force JOS out of the country within twenty-four hours. He reminded everyone that it was because of him that JOS was permitted to remain in Ethiopia. But, he asked, what difference did it make? What did it give Ethiopia as a whole? "It is only a drop in a very large body of water," he said. "If you add one drop to Lake Tana, does that change the volume?" He brought no specific charges, he simply blamed JOS in a general way for being involved in a secret emigration. That alone sufficed to terrorize the Jewish workers—they understood its implications. He denounced us for allegedly discriminating against the non-Jews of Ethiopia. Then he turned on Derso, the secretary of the workers' association, and said, "You, if you make any more trouble, I'll break your legs."

But Melaku was unable to single me out on a specific personal charge. Instead, he ordered the chief of Public Security to tell me to resign and leave Gondar. On Thursday, I received a call from him. He asked me to come to his office.

"I'm busy," I said.

"It will only take ten minutes," he answered.

I went. In his office he told me that I was involved in instigating people to leave the country.

"Are you sure?" I asked.

"Yes," he said.

"If you're sure," I said, "then I'm a criminal. If I'm a criminal, then why do you allow me to sit here?"

"You can count on it," he said. "I'll get you and kill you." Then he listed all of my faults again and told me I had to resign.

"I'll tell you what my real fault is," I said. "I don't buy whiskey for my bosses and invite you. And I don't feel comfortable sitting with Melaku the way Kabeda does.

"You know," I continued, "I wanted to ask a question yesterday that was too hard to ask during the meeting. So I'll ask it now. My friend Major Melaku—you know Melaku was my classmate—once had good things to say about JOS. I remember being at a meeting when he said that JOS will benefit all of Ethiopia. Well, I wonder about something. I have been against the exploitation of JOS. I have fought the people who would have stolen property from JOS for their own use. Doesn't this make me a loyal Ethiopian who is working for the good of all the people? I work for the 'trodden mass', including Falashas. Did anyone ever hear me say that only Jews can use the road that JOS built? The JOS program is a development program that benefits everyone, it is for communal use. Now I take two non-Jews into each of my training programs. In the future I'll be able to take more. Before I came, when there were no non-Jews in vocational programs, did anyone worry about that? Did Kabeda?"

He ignored me. "Resign or I'll kill you," he said.

"Do it now," I said, and walked out.

I went back to my office and told Yakov and the Jewish workers there what had happened, and that it had become too difficult for me to remain. One of the workers said, "Don't resign here. If you do, you won't be protected." My connection with JOS was my most important protection; if I had resigned in Gondar they could have grabbed me quickly. Without the political power of JOS behind me, they would never have let me leave the province. This worker had heard talk among his non-Jewish friends. "If you do resign, you must do it in Addis, not Gondar."

I called Daniel Mendes and went to stay in Addis Ababa with my wife and children. The workers in Gondar kept calling me about various projects and I told Mendes about the phone calls.

"Why is it that they don't call me?" he asked. For the first time, he realized that I was accepted in a way he was not.

"Why don't you ask them?" I said. "But, remember, I'm in Gondar all the time and you're not." The answer didn't satisfy him.

One of the Jewish teachers who had been jailed and tortured came to Addis with a *kes* affiliated with the school. They were being harassed by the Gondar Public Security, so I had arranged for them to be transferred out of Gondar. "You're an idiot," Mendes said. "You're taking them away from me, trying to make them more loyal to you."

That was the last straw. I resigned on the spot. On a Friday, I got work in a government department. It wasn't hard for me to get the job in Addis, far from the provincial government of Gondar where my name had been tarnished.

But the teacher and the *kes* showed up at my home, sent by Mendes. They were supposed to be mediators, to smooth the way and persuade me to return to the program.

"I wish you had never come to work for JOS," the teacher told me. "Then we never would have gotten to know you. But we have come to know you and to love you. Now is not the right time for you to leave. Things are too difficult. We are trying our best; we are united, but we need you. We'll work together and risk death together," he said. "But before we die, we'll buy mules and go to Tavari." Tavari was on the way to the border. He was saying that we would disappear and go home to Jerusalem together. I was very moved.

"Do you really mean it?" I asked him.

"Yes," he answered. "There is no alternative."

"Okay" I said, "I've changed my mind." I was surprised by what he had said.

They told me that Mendes wanted me to go with them, so we could all meet and discuss the situation. This I agreed to on one condition. I wanted to see the rights of the Jewish workers made equal to those of the non-Jewish workers. I wanted Mendes to approve of this in principle and then act on it.

I went to Mendes's house. We sat up very late, talking.

"I'll take the responsibility, as far as the field work is concerned," I told Mendes, "as long as you remove Major Tesfa. He's a troublemaker. I don't want him around any more. But we can't just get rid of him, because then he'll work from the outside to harm all of us. Please, call him to Addis, and keep him here."

It was a mistake. What I had done was to give the non-Jewish workers more reason to work against us. Tesfa liked being in Gondar, away from his family responsibilities and able to spend time with other women. Being sent back to Addis made him feel his job was threatened. Ultimately, he mounted additional pressure against us in Gondar, by telephone from Addis. But Mendes had accepted my terms. He called Major Tesfa to Addis, and the same day I left for Gondar. We didn't want the Major to know that we had been together.

I worked for three weeks in the field before everything finally fell apart. My friend Yakov was now doing Tesfa's job, as well as his own. I had selected one of the best of the Jewish teachers from the government schools, a man named Belay Yonaton, to take over for me as head of the education department. I was training him so that I could assume the position of project head.

Everything seemed to be going well. But the woodworking teacher, who was chairman of the workers' association discussion forum, had been bought by Kabeda for 100 birr. He was waiting for the opportunity to provide evidence for Melaku.

It didn't take long for him to find it. The discussion forums were held on Thursday afternoons, and all of the JOS teachers and trainees were supposed to be brought in to participate. Ordinarily, they were picked up by a JOS car, but on this particular Thursday, not one of the cars returned from the field. At that time, there was no way to know if sabotage was involved. I only knew we were waiting in the JOS offices for the return of a car that never arrived; it was very tense and difficult.

The forum took place, nevertheless. When it was over, the car still hadn't arrived. Among the people who were supposed to have been picked up from a vocational school four kilometers away was the woodworking teacher who was the forum chairman. This teacher and others from the training centers came back to the offices on foot, and went straight to the political committee to accuse me of improper behavior. The forum chairman said that because I was a Zionist agent, I had sabotaged the discussion forum. There were three witnesses against me, three non-Jewish department heads who testified that I had not sent a car for them.

They had their evidence. By that evening it had reached Major Melaku's office, and I knew I was in danger. I couldn't even discuss it with Mendes because he was at a meeting elsewhere in Africa.

On Friday, I went to Ambober, and on my way back, I made a stop at a nearby hospital to pick up Yeshwork. Some three days earlier, Yeshwork's grandmother, who was also my friend Yakov's mother, had died. Yeshwork had been pregnant and lost her child after the funeral.

Yeshwork lived in an apartment constructed for JOS workers, about two and a half kilometers from the offices in Gondar. Yakov lived one door away from her, with the woodworking teacher's apartment in between. I had intended to bring Yeshwork home and then spend the evening with Yakov.

But at the hospital I was met by a biology teacher I knew who told me I would be arrested if I returned to Gondar. His information was good; he was a member of the political committee. After hearing this, there were not many places I felt I could go, so I continued to Yakov's. Because of his mother's death, he had visitors. We went into his bedroom to talk privately; he had already heard the news. He told me that things were very bad for both of us.

I had 420 birr in my pocket. I thought of going back to my office, where I had more money, but it was too dangerous. I was already saying goodbye to Ethiopia.

Yakov and I stayed alone, speaking very little. Because the situation was so tense and unhappy, we did not discuss matters as we normally would have done, but my mind did not stop working. I was so busy thinking and trying so hard to stay alert that I did not feel frightened.

I wanted to close my eyes and come up with a plan. Where to go? Where to go?

At first, I wondered if we could run to Addis Ababa, where there was no Major Melaku and no Gondar Public Security. Yakov was a gentle, conservative person and he liked that idea. Maybe it would be all right there, although, of course, we might still be caught and searched on the way. Deciding was very difficult. But when I closed my eyes and thought of going to Addis, everything seemed totally black. When I thought about going west, to the jungle, it seemed bright. In this way our decision was made—we talked a bit and kept quiet, spoke two or three words and were silent again. Our final understanding was that we had no alternatives. We had to run to the jungle in order to save our lives.

This was the beginning of our journey to the Promised Land.

My family was in Addis, a great distance away. Even though I couldn't get to them to say goodbye, I knew I'd been right not to bring them to Gondar. They were safer where they were. They had a place to live and my wife worked, so they wouldn't starve even without my income. It was far better not to involve them in my escape—I would only be risking their lives. The boys were too young to make the treacherous trip that Yakov and I had decided on. I felt the most important thing was for me to get out safely. If I died, I certainly would have been of no help to them.

In making my final decision, I understood that it would be a long time before I would see my family again. I had to hope that once I reached Israel, there would be some way for them to join me. It was a painful thing, but it had to be accepted. There was nothing else I could do.

Yakov and I called a taxi and traveled to a nearby town.

Within two months after we had fled from Ethiopia, several teachers were again arrested and JOS was thrown out of the country. It was a great loss not only to the Jews of Ethiopia, but to all of the people. JOS brought growth to the land, as well as education to the youngsters.

The central government of Ethiopia was cheated as far as JOS was concerned. The stories that were so negative about JOS came from the anti-Semitic administration of Gondar—from Major Melaku. And Melaku was pushed by the non-Jews from within JOS. Under other circumstances, things might have gone very differently. They should have. Today, not only is JOS gone from Gondar—so is Major Melaku as provincial head.

Sometimes it takes time and distance in order to be objective. Now I am able to look back on my experiences with JOS, from here in Israel, and analyze things a little differently. When I ran, I had no choice. I was being pursued. At the very least, I would have been jailed and tortured. It is possible I would have been murdered.

But I might have had another choice earlier; my own emotions may have helped to defeat me. It was hard not to be angry in my circumstances. Even today, as I recall how anti-Semitic the environment was in Gondar, the old anger rises in me. Because of that anger, I felt the need to fight. It seemed a matter of Jewish dignity and survival.

Perhaps the mistake I made was in thinking that I could only avoid defeat by winning. Maybe I should have swallowed my anger, controlled myself, and compromised for the larger good. Maybe I should have looked the other way part of the time.

Now it is easier for me to understand the JOS top administrators, those Jews who once annoyed me so much by not fighting hard enough. In their way, they were trying to be constructive by keeping the JOS program in the country. If they were passive, it was because they were afraid of what would happen tomorrow.

The irony is that ultimately the non-Jews who had attacked us regretted their actions. They also lost as a result of their behavior.

In spite of all the grief, I have never been sorry for having been involved. I only wish I'd had more time in Ethiopia with "my kids," the students. I wish there had been a chance to better prepare them for what came next—their *aliyah*, done the hard way. All of our efforts were for their sake.

Photographs

(1984-1986)

Ethiopian Jewish Life

This hut is an Ethiopian Jewish synagogue. It often nestles close to the edge of the village.

A *kes* (Jewish priest in English or *kohan* in Hebrew), trained at Melata-Minata, Ethiopia's holiest Jewish city, blows on the *shofar*.

A *kes* with his razor sharp knife completes the ritual slaughter of a sheep.

Holy men of a large synagogue in Gondar City, trained in Melata-Minata, take part in *Seg'd*. Because the Ethiopian Jews left Israel before 2 B.C.E., they do not celebrate Chanukah. *Seg'd* celebrates the desire of the ancient Persian Jews to return to the Promised Land.

Traditionally, Ethiopian Torahs are made of parchment and bound in book form. The one held by this *kes* is especially prized because it comes from Israel.

A *kes* summons villagers to worship at the small village synagogue. These people regard their Jewish heritage so highly, that any non-Jew who enters the village must be immersed in the waters of the *mikvah* (Jewish ritual bath).

There are no rabbis in Ethiopian synagogues, only Jewish priests, as was the case at the time of the First Temple in Jerusalem. This priest, or *kes*, contemplates a Hebrew prayer book.

Men and women attend synagogue services together in Ethiopia.
There is no physical separation between them but they do not mingle
in the synagogue. Young girls listen from the courtyard.

Jews were isolated in the Ethiopian highlands when the Talmud was written. But they do have the oral law which this *kes* recites.

Three young villagers attend a religious service with their *kes*.

In 1904, Jacques Faitlovitch came from Paris to study the Ethiopian
Jewish culture. He considered the people authentic Jews at a time
when this was an unpopular position. Faitlovitch devoted his life to
bringing them into the modern Jewish world. He established the first
school system for Ethiopian Jews. Boys from several villages attend
this Faitlovitch-inspired school near Gondar City.

Although a *kipah* (yarmulka) is not traditionally worn by Ethiopian Jewish men and boys, this youngster proudly wears his.

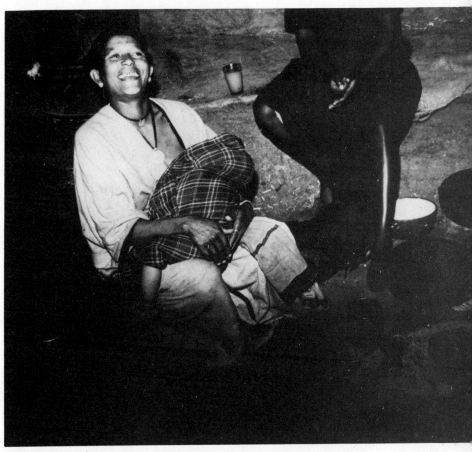

This Ethiopian Jewish woman holds her sleeping child in a *tukul*, **a round house made of straw. The** *tukul* **is always large enough for the family and has room for any 'stranger' who needs temporary lodging.**

Ethiopian Jews have always observed the laws of *niddah*, which requires a woman who is menstruating to live in a special hut called a *mergem-gojo*.

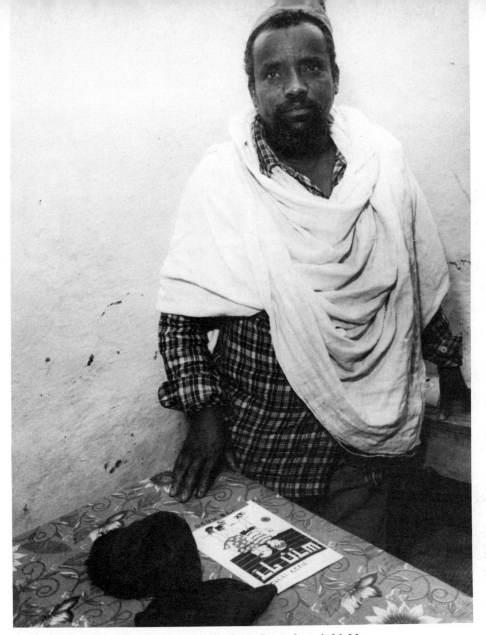

Any item from the Holy Land, especially from Jerusalem, is highly regarded. This man proudly displays his Hebrew language book.

News of an imminent visit from a Jewish Agency administrator, such as Shmuel Avraham, would spread through farmlands long before the official arrived.

While agriculture is a main staple of all villages, women also weave
and make pottery, which is sold to tourists. This woman, from the
small village of Wolleka, displays clay figurines and pottery.

In a poor country, male offspring mean power to a small community, so there is a unique relationship between father and son. As soon as a boy is able to walk, he goes with the older men to the fields, where he participates in the cultivation of the land.

A young girl will often marry at age seven, and live as brother and sister with her husband and his family for approximately seven years. The young husband then builds a *tukul* where he lives with his wife. This recently-married girl displays her imaginative carved sculptures.

After a first pregnancy, a young wife leaves her husband's home—and
his parents—and is instructed by her mother in child rearing.
For later pregnancies, she is considered "taught" and stays with her husband.

Life in an Ethiopian Jewish village is both hard work and fun. Here, a young man plays the *kirar,* a traditional string instrument.

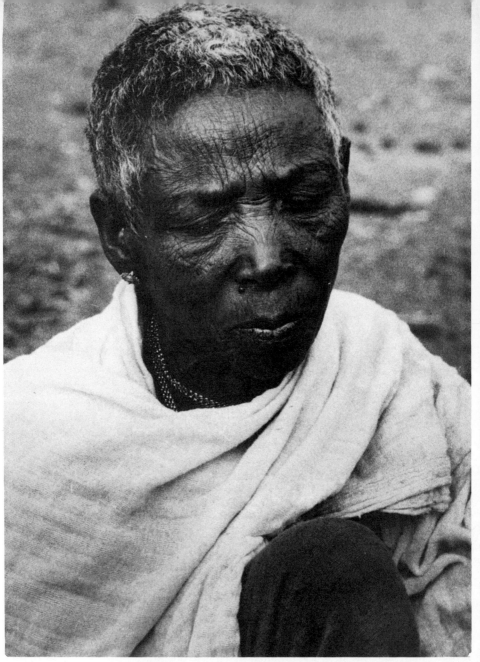

This elderly woman contemplates fleeing from the land of her birth in order to fulfill the lifelong dream of many Ethiopian Jews—*Seg'd*, or entry into the Promised Land.

6

*Escape
Westward*

Once Yakov and I decided to leave Ethiopia and drove into the rural area, I was able to relax and to concentrate on the details of our escape. The first village we reached was shabby, but it was a place where Yakov knew a few people, none of them Jewish. We felt that by going there we would be far away from the city of Gondar and thus would have no trouble finding shelter.

That first night, we slept in a very rundown house, although I wasn't really able to sleep. Not only was my mind in a turmoil, but the bed was infested with bugs.

The next day was Shabbat, but it was not easily observed there. Yakov slipped out of the village and found a young man—related to both of us—who was willing to guide us into the jungle. We felt it was important to use a relative in this situation, where trust was so essential.

I worried about involving a Jew, however; if he were caught with us things would go very hard for him. Still, we didn't seem to have any choice. The only way we could have relied on someone non-Jewish was if we were able to pay generously, but we had very little cash.

Our guide agreed to come back before dawn the next morning to take us out of the village and help us on our way to the jungle. He knew the route up to a certain point; we planned to meet with other relatives along the way who could guide us from one area to the next. I gave him thirty birr as encouragement. I had no fear he would betray us, but somehow it made it easier for me; I did not want to feel that I was using him unfairly.

There were a number of paths out of the village that would take us to the main road. The next morning, a Sunday, at about 4:30, we went to the meeting place we thought we had agreed on. But there must have been a misunderstanding: we waited and waited, but no one came.

I thought I remembered the way out from a time in my childhood when I had gone with my mother to visit an uncle and aunt. I also had some familiarity with the area as an adult—I had stopped at every Jewish village in Gondar, at one time or another, during my work in the field. We forged ahead on our own. I told Yakov I had an idea of what we could do if we were caught: "The village of your birth is in this direction. If anyone asks us, we can say that we are going there because it is the mourning week of your mother."

"And after we pass that village, then what?" he wanted to know.

"Then," I said, "we will be headed towards a village where there is a school. We will say we started out to spend the seventh mourning day at your birth village. First, we are heading towards the school because I have business there, and by nightfall we will go back to your village."

I don't think anyone would have cared what our excuse was. We were kidding ourselves, but it made us feel better to think we had a plan.

As we started our walk, our greatest fear was the arm associations. They were armed by the government and maintained checkpoints along the road we were planning to take. It was their job to guard against so-called antirevolutionaries; if they suspected anything, they were allowed to search you. We were worried we might get sent back to Gondar City if we got caught.

Luckily, that day happened to be Kibella, a Christian holiday. Early in the morning, everyone went to church and then returned home to celebrate with feasting and festivities; it was the day before the beginning of Lent, when there would be fasting. So no one paid attention to us on the road. We certainly hadn't calculated on this advantage and we thanked God that it happened.

About midday, we arrived at a Jewish village. Although I had relatives there, we headed directly for the village school. I did not want anyone to see us—it would have been dangerous for all of us.

We opened one of the classrooms and entered; a small child came in and saw us. He ran to tell others and someone, assuming we had come to the village for a school inspection, came to meet us. I told Yakov in English that we must pretend to be working in order to protect the people. Others from the village joined us. There were inquiries made, which I still remember, concerning the water supply, a clinic, and a wonderful synagogue that had been built there by JOS.

My relatives in that village had recently celebrated two weddings. The first one was held shortly after I had started work and I had been too busy to come. The second one had taken place just the previous week. I had been invited, but forgot all about it. Now, arriving in the village, I suddenly remembered, and it seemed the right thing to do to go and visit the family, chat, and celebrate. They had tella, a beer, which, normally, I never drank, but I sat and ate with them.

Everyone in the village wound up seeing us, which did not make us happy. Our fear was that if we only ate and visited with certain families, later they would be in danger for having associated with us. We realized that we had to visit with every family in the village so that none would be tarred by our presence and one family could not accuse another.

We spent a whole day visiting, moving from one household to the next. We drank quite a bit of the *tella* over the course of the day. I didn't feel intoxicated, because I was so tense; my body was working to its maximum, trying to be diplomatic and alert at the same time.

The last place we visited was the synagogue. There we made a donation of ten birr each, for our protection. I prayed, deep in my heart, and I wept.

"God," I said, "make the whole thing successful, up until Jerusalem. After I am in Jerusalem for a day, I will not care if I die." My prayers were very deep and long; I had never prayed that way before. Everyone who was in the synagogue became very quiet. As I prayed I was able to see my whole journey, as if it came in the name of God. I saw all of the problems, all of the difficulties I would suffer on the way, and I saw how I could cut through all of it and reach Jerusalem.

We returned to one of the houses we had visited earlier and suddenly I saw a boy I had known in Gondar, who seemed to be someone we could take with us as a guide. I found an opportunity to speak to him and he agreed to go with us. Just then, our first guide showed up—he had gone back to Yakov's house looking for us and finally followed us to this village. Now there were two boys with us, when a while before there had been no one. I was sure my prayer had been answered and that we would succeed.

The next question was how to disappear from the village. The people were so generous and polite that it was difficult to get away. We explained that we had to go back toward Gondar, to Yakov's birth village, for his mother's seventh mourning day. We hoped to walk in that direction merely for a kilometer or so and then to circle around. We did not want to lose what remained of the opportunity the Christian holiday afforded us—by the following day all the checkpoints would be manned again. We wanted to walk by night and be out of that area by morning.

But the villagers, not understanding our problem, wouldn't let us leave that easily. "You want to go without eating?" they said. They had slaughtered a sheep and prepared a meal for us without our knowledge. "Tomorrow," they said, "we will have mules and you will be able to go back to Yakov's village for the seventh day."

We had to recalculate. It would have been very bad to insult these good people; it was our final day with them, after all. Who knew what would happen in an hour or a day? We wanted to go away with love. We stayed and we ate. Actually, we were too upset to eat and only pretended to, but the warm feeling in that house, with everyone gathered, was lovely.

We lingered, and then met with our two young guides as if they were people with whom we had no special connection. But because I had so many relatives in the village who knew the guide from the other village, it was difficult to be inconspicuous.

That night, the man who had been our host wanted us to sleep inside his house. Since it would have been hard to slip out of his house unnoticed, we said we'd rather sleep outside. He told us that there was a dangerous dog in the area known to attack strangers; he was also concerned about robbers. Yakov was reserved; a polite man, he hesitated to refuse the hospitality that was being offered. But I was insistent. "No," I told our host, "we will sleep outside."

This made the man's wife suspicious. She took one of

the guides aside and asked what was going on. "Do they dislike us?" she asked. "Why would they prefer the outside to comfortable beds in the house?"

In order to avoid hurting her feelings, he told her. "They have to run away. They will escape at night."

The woman was shocked, but she was an intelligent lady. She told no one and convinced her husband to let us sleep outside. At the same time, she decided it would be a good idea if she sent her son along with us. At eleven at night, the two guides came to where we were resting, the young boy accompanying them.

At first, he told us that he would just go along for a short while. Later, when we had reached a certain point, he said he was going to go all the way with us. "I would love it," I told him, "but it would be dangerous for your parents." I knew that if we took their son it would have made them extremely vulnerable. However, at that point the boy stayed on with us.

We had a full night's walk ahead of us, and Yakov was already extremely tired. It had been a terrible time for him. He was just ending the mourning period for his mother. During the past week, he had spent many hours visiting with people and weeping and he had not slept. Then the beer he drank had made him drowsy. When we went outside for the early part of the night, I stayed awake, but he was so exhausted he fell asleep as he was still talking to me.

When the guides came, I woke him. His eyes opened, but he moved as if he were still asleep. Along the way, we saw someone off in the distance with a flashlight and our young guides became nervous and began to run. I ran after them. Yakov, suddenly alert, tried to follow. From behind me, I heard a horrible sound. Yakov's boot had slipped on a rock. I looked around and saw that his leg was dislocated and twisted at a terrible angle. I ran back to him and twisted his leg in the other direction—there was another horrible sound, but it was back in the right place. However, Yakov was in pain and for days he was unable to walk.

That night, the guides and I took turns carrying him, one of us holding him under each arm. It was a dark night with no moon. We went up hills and down hills. Even when we came to a gorge and had to go on hands and knees, we managed to carry him. It was a terrible night, but we managed to pass the dangerous checkpoint.

Early Monday morning we reached the next village, where Yakov's sister lived; no one had seen us. His sister was still in her mother's village, for the seventh day of mourning, but her husband was there and greeted us.

Yakov washed his leg, massaged it, and then rested. I wanted to leave again that night for another village on the far side of Gondar, where it would have been difficult for the Public Security men to reach us. The village was Tivari and it had a special signifigance for me: it is the place the Kfar Batya teacher had mentioned when he'd asked me to return to the JOS program. I hadn't forgotten.

Because of the holiday, I knew it would take a while before they discovered we were missing and came looking for us. I calculated that we had until Tuesday, and thought we should be well on our way to Tivari by then. However, it was very difficult for Yakov to walk.

Later that morning, a man came after us from the village we had just left. The father of the boy who had joined us wanted his son back. The boy understood his parents' danger and went willingly enough; actually, we were relieved that he was gone.

Yakov's sister, Devorah, his brother-in-law, Simcha, and their children, had only lived in the village for a month. Although it was Simcha's birthplace, family quarrels had driven them to Ambober. A feud had broken out between

Simcha's father and brothers and his uncle and cousins so serious it had caused a rift in the village, with one group living in the upper village and one in the lower. Only very recently, because of a wedding that was planned, had mediators brought the two sides of the family together, and there was still a great deal of tension.

A difficult political situation in Ambober had made Simcha and Devorah decide to come back to their home village. Because they had just returned, the *tukul* they were using was a poorly built one full of holes. Anyone could see in from the outside, which made it rather dangerous for us.

However, Simcha didn't want us to leave; he asked us to wait until Devorah returned. Not only would she prepare food for our long journey, he told us, but we would still be in the village for the wedding the following day. But he understood it was best if we were not seen; so we left the village during the day and hid in the jungle, returning at night to eat and sleep.

We were outside of the village on Tuesday, when the wedding took place and guns were shot off in celebration. Because of the way the village was constructed, with a rise on one side, we were able to hear everything clearly from our jungle hiding place. I listened to the dancing and laughing and paid attention to the sound of the guns exploding.

On Wednesday, Devorah and her son returned from her mother's village. She told us that on Tuesday, Kabeda had come to Gondar to pay salaries and had realized Yakov and I were missing. He thought that we might have gone to Yakov's birth village for the seventh day of mourning and sent people there looking for us. When he found out we were not there, he alerted Public Security. A report had gone to the police and they were now out looking for us.

I realized that they couldn't be far behind. Their network of communications was good and, in fact, they did come close to catching us. We were now in a dangerous area without transportation, moreover we had been seen in the village on Sunday. Although we could be reached only on foot, it wouldn't be terribly hard to trace us. I was afraid that vulnerable fellow Jews would be used against us to reveal our whereabouts. I was determined not to be caught and tortured by Major Melaku; I preferred to keep running—it would be better to take the chance of being killed along the way.

The police sent a Jew into the village where we were hiding, who pretended he had come to join in the wedding festivities. He carried a message, which he said was from a Jew in the Teda area to a Jew in that village. The message was: "Now is the time that we will have a belt." To have a belt is to have pants; to have pants is to be a real man. The implication was that Yakov and I, having the upper hand, had reduced the authorities to less than real men. Now was the time for the people in this village to show themselves to be real men by catching us.

Repeating a story calculated to destroy us, the man also said we had stolen 6 million birr from a government bank. Once the word went out to the professional bandits— the *shiftas*—that we were carrying a large sum of money, it would be the end for us. "If you have them killed along the way, the government will excuse you and will reward you."

The villager who received the message was the groom's father, who had not been on good terms with Simcha. It suited him to make trouble for Simcha at the same time that he attempted to destroy Yakov and me. The man had contacts with *shiftas*, and he got in touch with them. There was no way for them to be sure we were in the village, but it was a good guess we were somewhere in the area near Yakov's sister.

I had told Simcha beforehand that staying in the

village would be playing with fire. "It's not like anything you've ever been involved in before. I don't want anyone to be hurt on my account. Please, let us run, try to avoid us, there's no point in keeping us here." But Simcha did not want to let us go.

He intended to serve as our guide for the next leg of our journey. He knew he had to be seen at the wedding first or his absence would be noticed immediately, and there would be a strong suspicion as to where he had gone. So he asked us to remain for a few more days. Of course, this also pleased Devorah—it was important to her to spend more time with her brother.

On Thursday, we were hiding outside the village, when Simcha's son came to tell us that an old woman from a near-by village had come into their house as a visitor. Simcha wanted to know if we minded. Of course, we did. The possibility of a leak of information was too great, even though it might be done innocently. It would be dangerous for the people who were helping us.

Simcha arranged for us to go to his brother's house that night. Four of us went: Yakov, myself, and our two guides. We ate there and Simcha's brother asked us to sleep in his house. I was worried and refused; I needed to be certain we would have a way out and I knew that the longer we stayed the more problems there would be.

"Find a place outside for us to sleep," I said. "We can't sleep inside any more." I was feeling very closed in.

There was a wonderful place to sleep outside. Because the village was troubled by bandits who came at night and stole property, Simcha's brother had built a bed up in a large tree, so as to be able to scout the area from above. You could look out and see everything, without being seen. The only problem was that if you were discovered, you were caught with no way out.

The four of us spent the night in that tree. It was the middle of the night; there was bright moonlight. The others were fast asleep and I was dozing—I did not feel safe enough to sleep soundly. Suddenly, a small dog began to bark furiously and I jumped awake.

In the moonlight, I saw a man circling Simcha's *tukul*, peering in where he could. He had long hair and a scarf tied around his head: the mark of a *shifta*. In his hands he held a kalatchnikov, a sophisticated, Soviet-made, automatic rifle.

While I watched, I remembered something that had happened during the day. We had been hiding outside of the village while the wedding was still being celebrated. The sounds coming from the celebration were wonderful; there was dancing and I remember that I had listened carefully to the kinds of weapons that were being shot. Most of the weapons were very primitive, so that I heard a simple "boom-boom, boom-boom."

Then, suddenly, I became conscious of a new sound: "tat-tat-tat-tat." It was a kalatchnikov, which meant someone new was on the scene. He could have been either a soldier or a so-called antirevolutionary; they both used this automatic weapon. As I had listened during the day, there had been no way for me to guess which. Now, lying in the tree, I knew that the people who were after us had reached us. We had lingered in one place for too many unnecessary days.

It seemed to me that even though we were far away from Gondar, in an area of the highlands controlled by antirevolutionaries, there was a direct link from this *shifta* back to Major Melaku in Gondar.

I began to pray; however, this time it was not for myself. I prayed for the villagers who were now in danger. Perhaps we would get away—but after we left, they could be taken to prison.

We decided that on Friday morning we would move to a village that was not Jewish. Everyone was up very early. Devorah made coffee and prepared food for us to take along; she also gave us a small donkey for carrying it.

Before we could go, however, they had to perform a *woof,* a ritual that would give us a sign of our future. Before embarking on a trip, these people go outside, listen for the call of a particular kind of bird, and then wait for the bird to fly by. If the bird comes from the right, it means that you will succeed in your venture; if it flies from the left, you won't; if it flies from behind, you will die.

The bird call they heard was from the right direction; we would succeed. Although I had no faith in such a thing, I later wondered if one reason we did succeed was because these people believed we would. What I believed is that if we succeeded it would be because we had prayed.

Leaving was difficult. The people wanted to say a leisurely farewell and they couldn't be blamed. Who knew if we would ever see each other again? Devorah cried because her mother had died only a week before, and now her brother, adored by the family, was going far away.

In another situation I would have appreciated this slow goodbye, but I remembered what I had seen during the night. I didn't want to terrorize these good people, yet all I really wanted to do was run from there as quickly as I could. I felt the need to make up for the days we had lost by staying too long in that village.

Simcha and his brother came with simple firearms, to accompany us and be our guides. Simcha's son also came along, as well as one of the original young guides who was going to go all the way with us. The other young guide turned back at this point. I walked alongside Simcha, rushing as much as I could. No one else in our group was as driven as I was to get out quickly.

Our two guides, Simcha and his brother, each carrying one of the guns, spread out for our protection—Simcha in front leading the way, and his brother at the rear. I bumped against his leg as I walked along because of my constant impulse to bolt and run. There was only one main road we could take out of the village. It went up and down hillsides and there was one high spot, shortly beyond a crossroad, which gave control of the entire area. As we approached that strategic high point, a bird flew out from our left, made a series of strange noises, and flew on to the right.

Simcha was shocked. He stopped to make sure his gun was properly loaded. "Ah," he said, *"HaKadosh, Baruch Hu".* He saw the bird as a sign from God. "Get down!" he told us.

And I knew that the *shifta* with the kalatchinkov I had seen during the night had to be up ahead on the top of the hill. It would have been the logical place for him to wait for us, but I did not see him. While off to our right, that crazy bird did not stop his cry.

Then Simcha changed his mind about the direction we should take. He broke off a branch from a tree and left it as a marker for the other members of our party, who followed behind. They would understand that they shouldn't continue on the road as we had planned, but should turn to the right along the crossroad.

Eventually we reached a Christian village where Simcha had an acquaintance. No one else thought so, but I worried that the *shifta* with the kalatchinkov was tailing us. I was the only one who had seen him clearly at night and I understood from his eyes that he was a crazy, determined man. As we moved away, I thought about this man, and considered what his next move might be. I knew who he was. Back in Gondar I had heard about him and his six *shifta* brothers.

We were taken to a house in the village and gracious-
ly received. As the rest of our group came in, they kept looking backwards as they walked. I saw that and knew
immediately that they had been followed. They came into
the compound of the house we were in, and then I saw the
man I had seen the night before: his features, the scarf on
his head, the way he held the gun. The image was all clear
in my mind—it was him. Two other men were with him—
sure enough, two of his brothers, all with similar complex-
ion and features.

"Please," I said to the man of the house, "don't let them
in here. Find someplace else for them." I knew that according to our culture he would give them a place to stay if they
needed one. The owner of the house gave them a small *tukul*
some distance away.

We were given some food and drink and talked for a
while, but things became very uncomfortable. Some years
ago Simcha had known the father of these *shiftas*. In those
days, he had been a wealthy man; his seven sons only became *shiftas* after the revolution, when their land had been
confiscated. As a boy, Simcha used to visit the father, who
was so fond of him that he thought of him as family.

Now, while we were eating, Simcha went to see the
three *shiftas* in their *tukul*. He greeted them and told them
he was escorting us to some nearby mineral waters for ther-
apeutic treatment.

"You are lying," they said to him. "We know they have
stolen 6 million birr. But we are not greedy. All of us here
ought to share it." Simcha came back very upset; he knew
the story wasn't true. I wasn't even able to pay him for his
assistance to me.

Then I discovered that unknowingly we had entered
right into the territory of the *shiftas*. They had second families in the village; in fact, the daughters of our host were

their second wives.

I still hadn't figured out how that story of the 6 million birr had been carried exactly to the village where we were. But however it had happened, it seemed to me that now we were trapped. I decided that at least we could make it obvious that we weren't carrying the money.

Yakov carried a bag. He had put some antimalaria capsules and some underwear in it before we had left his house. I hadn't come from my own house, and so I was not carrying anything. I had put a carton of Winston cigarettes in Yakov's bag, and nothing more. Women from the village were sent in to the house to serve us and to act as spies. I opened the bag in front of them and spoke to Simcha. "Six million birr? Where do they think we carry it? There is nothing in here. We are anti-Major Melaku. We know that the people in this area are anti-Major Melaku. We are brothers."

The women looked at me with widened eyes; I had clearly succeeded in agitating them. They served us coffee, and then ran off to report what I had said, returning later to watch us again.

We had to get out of there and I was prepared to run at any cost. But now the *shiftas* were ready to negotiate using Simcha as intermediary. They came down from their ransom of 6 million birr to 3,000. A thousand birr was the going price for a life in that area—what was paid as compensation when someone was killed, so that there would be no blood revenge. They wanted a thousand birr for each of us trying to escape: for me, Yakov, and our young guide.

We did not have anything near 3,000 birr. I had about 400. We were as good as dead. We had no choice but to try and cheat the *shiftas*.

We put together all our cash. Yakov had about 500 birr;

from my pocket there was 420 birr; our guide had 60 birr. We couldn't cheat with this—what was there, was there. But we had merchandise. There were two watches. I said one was worth 350 birr and the other 250 birr. And we set a value of 500 birr on one of our firearms.

We gave all of this as an advance on what we owed. In addition, Simcha stood as our guarantor, giving up his gun as a pledge that we would deliver the rest of what we owed. The owner of the house then served as guarantor for Simcha, which made it possible for him to have his gun back for as long as he was our guide. Our host pledged that Simcha would return to surrender it.

I was feeling very angry about having been trapped in this way. If it were still Tuesday instead of Friday, this would never have happened, and I began to wonder on whom we could rely. But the *shiftas* told us we could go and I thanked God for that.

They accompanied us for a while and as we walked, I noticed that my physical appearance had intimidated them. They said that I looked like a trained soldier and they kept their distance from me. But after I had removed my jacket in the warm sun, they moved closer to me; they had suspected I was carrying a pistol inside it.

Carefully, I began to ask them questions, trying to find out how they had come to trap us. I assured them that I was not angry. They told me that two weeks earlier the government had burned their property and taken their cattle away; they had then received a message saying they would be forgiven by the authorities and would get their cattle back if they "acted like men" and came after us. The message had come from a JOS man; it was someone I knew.

I had done favors for the man who had sent the message. I was greatly agitated and kept thinking that this was not yet the end of what Major Melaku would try.

We were approaching a large river called the Guang. The *shiftas* said goodbye and turned back, watching us from a high point as we continued on our way. Once they were gone, Simcha told us that he had no intention of surrendering his gun to them after he returned. He felt it would be dangerous and he was furious with the way they had acted. After all, they had grown up with him.

It was a hot day. We approached the bank of the river— and suddenly a large snake began moving towards us. How it moved past Yakov and the donkey, I do not know, but it came directly at me. I was wearing bright orange boots of heavy leather which had been brought from Geneva for the JOS field workers. In an instant, the snake had wound itself around my leg and sunk its fangs into my boot. Luckily, the leather was thick enough to prevent the fang from penetrating to my foot, but when I looked down I saw that the leather had turned black where the poison had spread.

Then the snake slithered on to the ground and turned over. I took my walking stick and hit it so hard it divided in two. I was in such shock that at first I didn't realize what I had done. The tail end of the snake twitched; the head seemed still alive—its black tongue flicked in and out, and it looked at me with its terrible eyes. I stepped on its head with my full weight and it exploded, splattering out.

One of the *shiftas* up on the hill saw it and called out to me that it was good luck.

We ate some of the food Devorah had given us and drank from the river. Then we crossed it and moved on. By nightfall we had arrived at a non-Jewish village. Simcha was friendly with people who lived there.

It was Shabbat; we rested for the day and prayed. Our prayer was that we would reach Jerusalem peacefully.

There was a farm association nearby, whose chairman was a member of the family Simcha knew. He understood very well what we were doing, but would not expose friends. He politely asked us not to go out of the house—he did not want to be caught helping us.

We ate. They tried their best for us, but the food was not kosher. However, we had no choice—it was better to eat than to starve.

We had planned to leave the next morning, but our host told us we couldn't go until we received a sign from the birds, and the birds weren't ready. "Oh," I said, "Unless the birds are finished in Armachiho, Shmuel cannot go out?" Everyone laughed, but this was what they really believed and I wasn't a bit happy about waiting for the birds.

I was worried about our guides—Simcha and his brother. I said to them, "The *shiftas* are going to make trouble for you if you don't pay the guarantee or surrender your gun. Besides, your feelings have changed so that you cannot live near these people comfortably any more. Please, go back now and get your families and go out of the country. Or, at the very least, leave the area, go to lower Armachiho, to a liberated antirevolutionary area."

They said they were willing to go on and then, along the way, decide whether to go all the way out with us. But I decided that they had to go back. They were far from their original area and far from their families. Only one of them was familiar with the territory we were headed toward. I wanted to see them return home quickly and get their families and save themselves.

They did go back but, not alert to the dangers, they moved slowly without protecting themselves. It turned out exactly as I had feared. The security forces had traced our route through the villages and figured out who was also absent from a village when we left it. Our guides were caught, put in prison, and tortured. For six months they suffered. When I heard about this, after I was out, it sickened me, but there was nothing I could do.

There is a saying of Mao Tse-tung's that goes, "A friend of my friend is my friend, an enemy of my friend is my enemy, and the enemy of my enemy is my friend." But it certainly did not work that way in Armachiho. We were running from Melaku, and the *shiftas* had been destroyed by Melaku—we were all equally opposed to Melaku. Yet, the *shiftas* were not willing to protect us on that account. In fact, they participated in exposing Simcha and his brother to the government, and once Simcha was in jail, they came at night and took all his property, in retaliation for the fact that he had not surrendered his gun to them when he returned to the area.

Once Simcha and his brother had headed back, we were left in the village without guides and without money. However, I told the people we were staying with that if they would provide guides, we would pay. Of course, I didn't tell them it was safer for non-Jews, which was why I wanted them.

Two people came and told us they would lead us out. "How much do you want?" I asked.

"Four hundred birr," they said.

"Okay," I told them.

On Sunday the birds didn't cooperate; we couldn't go. On Monday, finally, the birds were ready to give the sign—it was all right. Our new guides brought two donkeys with them. There was a shortage of salt in the area, and they were going to use the 400 birr to buy large quantities of salt in Sudan and then return to sell it.

Shortly after starting out, we came again to the river we had crossed on Friday. As we had done before, we took the time to wash ourselves, but now, for the first time, we also washed our clothes, which was most pleasurable.

Another good thing happened because I washed my clothes—in a pocket of my jacket I discovered money I hadn't noticed previously. On that very last workday in Gondar, I had stopped for coffee in a hotel before setting out for Ambober and had bought a pack of cigarettes, paying with a 100 birr note. The change from the 100 birr had been in my jacket pocket all of this time. I was glad I hadn't found it sooner or I would have given it to the *shiftas*.

We put our clothes back on, still wet, and remained by the side of the river for a while. Then we continued on our way, crossing for the second time.

We didn't travel far; in about two hours we came to a village where we met a wonderful non-Jewish family. I had heard of them before, because of important things they had done in helping others. The son of the family had been killed as he fought with antigovernment forces near the border, so they were fiercely anti-Melaku. The man was a priest, but he did weaving. Almost always this is something the Jews of Ethiopia did; most non-Jews would not: "Weave? Like a Falasha?" To me, it showed that he respected our culture, and I loved him for it.

At night, we didn't sleep in the house; we were taken outside beyond the field to sleep. There was a man with a gun who stood guard over us. It was wonderful, because we were protected. I was fearful of snakes, however, and I thought that one might come up from the earth, even while the man watched.

The next morning, Tuesday, one of the sons of this family asked me if I would like him to buy me cigarettes. I had already tried the local tobacco. It grows wild, and some had been brought to me. I rolled it myself in old newspaper, but it almost killed me when I smoked it. "You can get cigarettes?" I asked him.

"Yes," he said. "Mohammed goes in to Gondar to buy

them and sell them to the antirevolutionaries." The place was full of antigovernment people who had come from all over the country to "liberate" the area.

I gave him 10 birr. "Bring me what you can," I told him. "Nasty ones, cheap ones, I don't care."

He came running back in a few hours, without cigarettes but with new information. He was a member of EDU, the underground party that was at that time trying to reestablish the rule of Haile Selassie's line, and he had connections. His face was completely changed. He was angry—and fearful. He said that fifty soldiers and a military district governor, from a distant area, were coming to search for two men. The two men, of course, were myself and Yakov. It was clear that high government officials were involved.

Major Melaku had wired a message about us to three border areas, Hummara, Abderafi, and Metema, which were all controlled by the army, and people had been waiting for us along all the main roads of those border territories. We weren't so stupid that we would have walked the roads openly; we would have gone at night as we approached the border. But it actually turned out to have been fortunate that we were delayed along the way. Had we gone directly, we would have been caught. When we hadn't shown up, they had decided to fan out back into the areas controlled by antigovernment people, until they either spotted us or convinced someone to tell them where we were. They were coming from the direction that we were headed toward.

The army also hoped to accomplish something else while sweeping through the antigovernment area. Such things as large oxen were smuggled across the border regularly and sold in Sudan by the antirevolutionaries. Officials wanted to control this at the same time as they looked for us.

My mind started to work furiously again, and the old priest and his wife began praying. Then the young man—who was very small in size, but was very much a true man—went to his *gotah*, and put the simple gun he had been using down into it and pulled out a very sophisticated machine. It was all iron, Chinese-made.

He ran outside with this gun and hid behind a shelter of branches known as a *gudib*, which had been prepared beforehand as camouflage, in case it was ever needed it. A man wanted by the government, he was always alert. He waited there, where he could not be seen, ready to shoot anyone who approached. He didn't know how much damage he could inflict before he was hit himself, but he knew at least he would die while trying to protect his family.

One of the guides became very agitated: "My children, what will happen?" This was not the usual behavior for a guide who was responsible for protecting us. He was supposed to hide his fear, remaining brave even in the face of danger. I judged him to be a weak person, from whom we could expect very little. But we kept him because he knew the way out and we needed him. Besides, we were not likely to find a better guide—people in that region tended to get particularly nervous in the presence of police or government officials.

I waited until the old man had finished his prayer and then simply asked, "Which is our way out?"

He showed us. "This way and in that direction."

"But aren't the soldiers coming this way?" I asked him. "What would happen if we went round about and out the other way?"

"Ah!" he said, because he suddenly was reminded of something. He called one of the guides, "Ato Hailu, do you remember the time we went by this road and across the back to here?" They knew each other, the guide was a relative of the old man's wife.

The guide thought for just a second. "Ah! Yes!" he said. He turned to me and Yakov. "Let's run out of here. Now is the time."

Quickly the guides loaded the donkeys and we left. Up on a hillside to the right of the house, a large wild goat was grazing. A man in a nearby house, not aware of our presence, shot the goat, and it came tumbling down the hillside to our right. The old priest was watching us leave and saw what happened. "You are saved," he said. "There will be no more obstacles, not ever again." The *woof* was in our favor.

Now we walked the long way around, in order to avoid the army. We went northward, down a hill and far from the main road, and came to a river which snaked its way back and forth across our path. In the course of one and a half days, we had to cross it eighteen times. Then we found our way back to the main route, past the area where the army was moving, and continued going for several days more.

On the road, we met oxen merchants from lower Armachiho who were going toward the Sudanese black market. It was their practice to buy oxen cheaply in their area and sell the animals at a high price across the border. Then they would buy salt inexpensively at the border and return to sell it at inflated prices.

They spoke the original peasant Amharic—which differs from the peasant Amharic of Gondar—with a little Arabic from the Sudanese merchants thrown in. Because they moved back and forth between different areas, their dress was a mix of styles. They wore some Sudanese clothes and some Ethiopian peasant clothes, with a touch of modern style.

We traveled with a small group of these oxen merchants. Their presence gave us protection and made us less visible. Because our guides were local people, these merchants knew them. This made it safer for us: even though the merchants suspected we were not peasants, they wouldn't touch us.

At one point we came across *shiftas* who were tying up some merchants. That's when I changed into peasant's clothes brought from the village. I had left on my boots, which were not like peasant shoes, and one of the guides advised me to take them off and load them on a donkey. The black plastic peasant shoes I had to wear were lightweight and had ventilation, but were very hot. The clothes were not only dirty and smelly, they were lice-ridden.

I tried my best to pass as a peasant, but it was almost impossible for me. Even though my skin was darkened black from the sun, it was soft and smooth, not rough and worn like a true peasant's. Unlike the peasants, I wore underwear. Once I was checked for that—someone pulled away my pants and looked to see what was underneath. And my speech, no matter how hard I tried, was never really peasant's speech, the accent was wrong, so that even though I was with others who were rural people, I was repeatedly singled out as someone from the city.

Or I would be asked if I was from EPRP—Ethiopian People's Revolutionary Party (called "antirevolutionary," but in fact an antigovernment revolutionary party). Depending on the area we happened to be in, sometimes I would say "yes" and sometimes "no." I always said no when I was sure I had been identified as someone from the city.

We had traveled so far and long that we had now come into a semidesert area—for hours on end no water was available. We carried water with us, first from the river we had crossed on our first days out, and later from waterholes we found along the way. Sometimes our water was gone long before we came to another source; at other times we suspected the water was polluted and then we had to take our chances. We heard stories about people who had died from polluted water.

To avoid checkpoints, we often walked at night. The people who manned them were savage and would have killed us quickly. When we approached the main road, we worried about being picked up by government people, but we couldn't go too far from the road. Although we were using a compass, we were afraid we might totally lose our way.

One very hot day something happened I will never forget. A merchant had pointed out a bird that knows how to locate honey. I was curious enough about this to stop and watch what was going to happen. The bird flew straight to a large tree and just sat there, squawking. The merchant split the tree open and found a beehive inside—in that terrible heat, the bees were in a stupor and unable to sting. He pulled the honeycomb out onto a rock, cut off a large piece, and handed it to me. I loved honey and took it gladly. But in the heat it made me incredibly thirsty. I felt crazy, it was more than I could bear.

Because of how I suffered, we changed our direction to look for water. On the way, we met a man who pointed out a place. We didn't know it then, but he was a Jew on a mission, and I have since met him in Israel.

We went where he directed us, and as we approached, the odor was unbearable. We didn't see any water, there was just a terrible smell. The land was flat and soft. In that area, a riverbed sometimes flooded over, and the water was beneath the surface. You had to dig down with your hands and walking stick to find it, which was not difficult. Lions in the area were able to dig with their paws to get to the water. They would drink, and then urinate nearby so that their urine seeped down through the porous soil back to the water, which is why the area smelled the way it did.

We had no choice; we had to have water. I got down on the ground and dug through the urine-soaked soil until I found dirty water, using my dirty clothing to filter out the impurities that were floating in it. I placed my clothing over the water surface and sucked the water through, holding my nose so that I couldn't smell it. I drank and I drank that way. Then the others did the same. Incredibly, we did not get sick.

We rested for a short while and came back to drink again, before going on our way. Within an hour, I was horribly thirsty all over again. I took a leaf off a branch and chewed it, hoping to, at least, have some saliva. My mouth was completely dry and I was becoming dehydrated.

Five hours later we arrived at a place where there was flowing water. Bugs flitted here and there on the surface and fish darted below. This life told us it was clean water. I immersed my body in it all the way up to the top of my head. Then I raised my nose above the water level, opened my mouth, and just let the water flow into me, swallowing mouthful after mouthful.

When I left the water and stood in the heat, I lost it all. It was too much for me and I became violently sick. I drank a second time and was sick a second time.

I went back a third time. This time I held what I drank. Then I took off my stinking peasant's clothes and washed them in the water. There was no soap, of course, but I did manage to make those clothes smell like the water, which was a blessing.

All of us were exhausted, and so we slept for half an hour and then our guides brought us food. In spite of my first anxieties about them, they had turned out to be good people who cared for us well. Many evenings when we stopped to rest, they washed our legs, and massaged our muscles deeply, so that we could sleep in a relaxed state and be refreshed by morning.

Along the way, we had trouble passing urine, perhaps because there was no water in our bodies. It was a terribly painful business. The guides helped us with this too, with a substance called *chilka*, which had been prepared for us in the second village we had been in. Special black seeds were roasted and then ground into a powder. When we had difficulty, the guides mixed this powder into water and once we drank that, we were fine.

For many days we continued at night, in order to avoid the checkpoints. Then on the last day we reached the area between Metema and Abderafi, near the Guang, the big river we had crossed twice before. When we crossed it again we would be in Sudan. It was 1:00 a.m. when we approached this final border. There was the sound of a truck in the distance, and sometimes we could see lights from afar. Our guides told us where we were and that the activity was coming from Sudan.

Usually Yakov tired quickly, but on this night he was the most energetic of us all, as if he had finally accepted where we were going. He reached the river first, while we lagged behind. When I got there, I just fell down and slept. I remember that the guides went down to the river and got water and made *chilka* for us to drink, and that when they washed my legs the water was cold. Then they massaged me, and I slept without knowing where I was. That night, while Yakov was so energetic, I was exhausted. And it is here, while I slept, that I dreamt my last dream about my father.

Early the next morning, I awoke feeling confused. Merchants who had come from different areas were sitting around near me: it was a marketplace and from the other side Sudanese came to buy things. I had seen Sudanese

people before, but now I was still half asleep and the atmosphere felt very alien to me. The Sudanese from the
south and west are very big people, very dark-skinned. They
wear strange-looking, long white robes with wide sleeves,
called *jelebiya*. I stood up suddenly, remembering that I had
just escaped and that I was at the Ethiopian border.

At that point, a man who had been standing with the
Sudanese saw us and ran away. He caught our attention as
he ran and we realized that we knew him—he was from
Gondar, someone I suspected of being on Melaku's payroll.
He returned with a Sudanese local authority who spoke in
Amharic. This Sudanese man might have lived in Ethiopia
for years; his grammar was correct, but his pronunciation
was strange. He did not seem concerned about the fact that
he was on Ethiopian soil, in this area no one bothers with
a careful distinction.

We were all under a big tree, where the merchants un-
loaded their wares. Yakov covered his face and pretended to
sleep; the boy who was with us was well disguised; our
guides blended in with the others. I was the one who was
caught. The eye of the Sudanese man had fallen on me.

"You! Man, where are you from?"

I smiled at him, and adjusted my speech to sound like
a peasant. I told him I was from the village that was my
guide's village. He asked me why I had come. I told him that
I was selling oxen.

"Where are they?" he asked.

"Over there," I said, pointing to some nearby oxen.

"They are mine!" the real owner of the oxen said. But
I spoke loudly to cover what he was saying, and the man
who was questioning me did not hear.

I ignored the man from Gondar completely, as if I did
not know him, and concentrated all my attention on the

Sudanese man. The Ethiopian Security man spoke to him in Arabic, which I do not understand. Then the Sudanese turned back to me.

"Are you from EPRP?" he asked.

"Me?" I said, "you are talking to me? I don't know what you are talking about. I am a simple farmer. I have come to sell oxen and buy salt."

"Will you pay taxes for the oxen?" he wanted to know.

"Of course, I will pay taxes."

"Do you have a pass from Mengistu Hailu Mariam?" he asked me.

"Why do you ask me? How about everyone else? Does anyone here have a pass? Of course, I don't have a pass. No one asked me about this when I was here before."

"Did you come here two years ago with stolen oxen and sell them?"

"I come here often, but I never steal anything. I am a low, respectful man, who does no wrong."

The two of them finally left our area and went off to see "my" oxen. Immediately, I told my friends that it was the time to run. I had in my pocket the money from the small donkey, which had been sold by Yakov and the guides while I still slept earlier that morning.

The guides were shivering. "Boys," I said, "I am the one causing this trouble. I am going to run, you follow me." It had happened a number of times that I had been the one to give myself away. Sometimes it was my appearance, but other times when I was tired I forgot to speak as a peasant.

I ran down to the big river, which I had to cross for the third and final time. If I had crossed right there, I would have been seen from the Ethiopian side, because there was a highpoint nearby where the oxen were kept. So I kept running along the river bank until I came to a lowland area that had a lot of trees, covering me from the Ethiopian side. I knew I was still exposed on the Sudanese side, and this worried me. I didn't want to attract attention, especially since I knew there was an army camp on the other side. I was also worried about crocodiles and other water animals that could get me as I tried to cross.

From the lowland area, I crossed the river, stepping on rocks that stuck out of the water. Tall grasses grew around the rocks in the middle of the river, and hidden in the grasses was a wild animal of some sort. As I went past, it let out a horrible shrieking noise. I slipped from the rock, and fell into the deep water. I went in, grabbed at a large rock, and held on. The weight of my wet peasant clothes pulled me down, but I managed to get back up. I squeezed the water out of my clothes, and continued to the other side.

As I approached the Sudanese side, there were cattle drinking at the edge of the river. They were startled by the sight of me, and immediately came forward with their horns lowered.

I might well have been killed, had not the owner of the cattle seen what was going on. He let out a strange cry, and the cattle turned back, just like that. I didn't know that cattle could be trained that way.

7

The Other Country

I stepped out of the water, onto Sudanese soil, and started walking without knowing where I was going. Soon I came to a simple village with houses made of straw. One building had a tin roof, in the modern style.

"*Dinkuan?*" I asked someone, using the Arabic word that I knew meant shop; the oxen merchants I had been traveling with had taught it to me. I was pointed in the direction of the building with the tin roof. Since I didn't know the language, I realized that all I was going to be able to say at the shop was one international word—"cigarette."

As I approached the shop, I was startled to see someone whose features looked Ethiopian. He was sewing, and he turned and looked at me.

When he began to speak, I was even more startled: he was obviously an educated man, who spoke a modern Amharic in a polite way. "Friend, what can I do for you?"

He was smoking, and without saying anything I stood and watched the smoke as it blew out of his mouth. He understood and gave me a small pack of ten cigarettes.

I sat, feeling dazed, and he began to speak to me. Not everything he said seemed clear, but though I was confused I was careful not to reveal anything. He asked me if I was with the EPRP. I didn't want to respond, because I didn't know what the right answer would be.

Instead I asked him where he was from. He told me he was from Tellemt, and that he was a member of EPRP. I knew where in Ethiopia the EPRP bases were, so then I was able to tell him I had come from another antirevolutionary area—Belessa—far away from where he had lived.

"Ah," he said, "like us, you dispersed?"

"Oh, yes," I told him, "long ago."

"Since when?"

"A month ago."

"And you are coming to here now?"

"Yes, I am sorry to say."

"No struggle?"

"No struggle."

I sat there and smoked the cigarettes, one after the other. When I finished the first pack, he gave me a second, and I smoked three more cigarettes from that pack. As the nicotine entered my system, I could feel myself getting better, so I felt able to analyze what was going on. He also gave me two cups of a wonderful spiced Sudanese tea, which helped me relax.

My only concern was for Yakov and the young boy, who had not followed yet. Without giving away any secrets, I told this man stories about our travels. He seemed so sincere that I trusted him enough to do this. I told him about the Sudanese man, and how I was afraid that my dear friends were in trouble with him.

"Here? You had this trouble here?" he asked. "This is EPRP territory. Don't worry. You go and look for them. If you think they will be in danger, I will go and get them out."

As I went back to look for Yakov and the boy, I saw them coming toward me, with the two guides. We returned to the Ethiopian man and he gave us a small *tukul*, with beds made of wooden frames and woven grass. It was the first time we had slept in beds in a long time. The Sudanese people who employed this man seemed to us both interesting and polite—they brought us fruit, bread, and drinks.

The Ethiopian money I had in my pocket was considered almost like dollars in Sudan and I suddenly felt rich. We changed the money we had to Sudanese currency, and asked the man if there was transportation to one of the refugee areas. He told us that there would be, in the morning, and he convinced the Sudanese to give us a small amount of additional money because he thought we were with EPRP.

In the morning, the five of us went to the refugee area. The offices of various antirevolutionary groups as well as that of the Ethiopian government were all maintained there. We didn't feel secure; we knew that Melaku's men were likely to have followed us.

Yakov and I, with the boy, decided to go to the Red Cross offices and register officially as refugees. Not all Ethiopian Jews did this. We went the morning after we arrived in the area and acquired refugee status—although we did not identify ourselves as Jews. We received identity cards and were entitled to certain benefits as refugees: we were allowed to be employed and were put on a list that made us eligible for visas to another country provided foreign sponsorship was available.

I expected to find Jews there as soon as I arrived, but it actually took five days of wandering before we located them. In the local United Nations office there was an Ethiopian translator who turned out to be the son of a professor I had studied with in Addis Ababa. When he spoke to me, something about his speech pattern reminded me of his father, so I asked him and found out who he was. I told him that his father had been my teacher; I did not tell him that I was Jewish. He told me his father was in London, and that he had also been in London and had come to Sudan to teach English and technology, serving as a translator as well.

This translator tried to be helpful. He interviewed people to establish a priority list for refugee resettlement in Canada and the U.S. The only place I wanted to go, however, was Israel, and so I avoided those interviews.

In my effort to locate the Jewish refugees, I asked the translator some roundabout questions: "I have a friend in Israel," I said, "and a brother in Paris, and an uncle in London. In Canada I have another relative. Can you let each of these people know where I am?" I hoped that his answer would lead me to Israeli agents nearby.

"I can reach your uncle in London," he said, "if you have an address. And in Paris and Canada, it is also possible. But I do not know anything about Israel."

By the sixth day, we found the Jews and joined them. With the assistance we received, we were able to pay our guides and send them on their way. Then we began to realize that the Jewish people were dying in the refugee camps, and that life there was painfully difficult. In the three months we lived there, we saw it all: poverty, starvation, disease, and death. It felt as if we had been there for years.

As all refugees did, we had to buy the cheapest food available—mostly vegetables. The problem was that most of the Ethiopian refugees were not familiar with the preparation of this food.

Sanitation was poor. There was a shortage of clean water for washing the vegetables, and few were aware of other ways that the germs on them could have been killed—using acidic liquids like lemon juice would have helped, for example. The refugees simply chopped them up, and ate them with salt.

Consumed this way, the vegetables were a primary cause of diarrhea. And diarrhea, especially amoebic diarrhea, led to dehydration. Medication was in very short supply, and since there was not sufficient drinking water available to compensate for loss of body fluids, many died—especially the children.

The refugees found themselves in a new area, contending with a new environment and culture. As they discovered that essential assistance was not available to them, tensions rose. When it came to sharing exceedingly limited resources, there was a breakdown of their communal traditions, causing confusion, and intense fear.

There was a particular family I will never forget. I found the wife walking around in a daze, carrying her dead baby. She didn't know that the child had died because she was so sick herself—her fever was exceedingly high. Twenty-four hours after I first saw her, she, too, was dead.

She and the child were buried inside the floor of the hut where the family lived. Proper burials were not possible. A few days later, the father of this woman was also dead. Her husband had been killed in a fight on the way to Sudan.

All this unnecessary death, the beautiful lives wasted, was ghastly and obscene. I saw it repeated over and over, and very little of what was happening made any sense. These poor people had come in hopes of reaching Jerusalem. Watching them die made me heartsick and brought me to the edge of despair.

From the refugee camp, I wrote letters and sent them through regular postal routes in a nearby town. I contacted JOS headquarters in Europe, a friend in Paris, an Ethiopian in Canada, and an American I had known who had been studying in Cairo and came to visit the Ethiopian Jewish community. All of this was possible because I always carried my little address book in my pocket. An Ethiopian-style book, made of plastic and designed like a closed wallet, it had survived all of the times it got wet and is still with me today.

I sent the letters during my first days in the camp, before I had found the Jews and discovered their misery. "Help us get out!" I wrote.

An American of influence in Chicago heard about me and tried to help, but couldn't. Others also tried, but couldn't. Finally all of the combined pressure had an effect. By then Yakov and I had moved to another area, but we were among those saved by the Israelis, at a time when many were still left behind.

Before I came into Israel, I became sick myself. We had to buy water, as that was the only way to get any, but the water we paid money for was polluted. As soon as I drank it, I knew: I could feel it burning all the way down. Then I was very sick. The pain was constant. An Israeli came for me and took me in a car. Almost immediately, he handed me a capsule to treat my condition. If I hadn't been saved at that time, I, too, might have been counted among the dead.

I left Sudan with the greatest possible relief, but swearing to remember what I had seen and to tell the world about it. Sometimes the memories threatened to overwhelm me, and I was driven the way I had been in those last days in Gondar.

Now the Jews are gone from Sudan, whether brought to Israel, returned to Ethiopia, or buried in the ground. Yet those who suffered there and what I saw of them will be with me the rest of my life.

8

Epilogue: Israel

Early in the summer of 1981, I found myself at Israel's Lod Airport with a group of other Ethiopian Jews redeemed from Sudan. At long last, we had come home to Jerusalem, and we all knelt to kiss the promised land. The moment was perfect in every detail; even the weather was beautiful.

I saw very quickly what a crazy place it was—cars going all about and people rushing here and there. Jewish Agency officials and two Ethiopian translators received us. We were taken to a room to rest and given something to eat and drink.

Soon, however, feelings I could not understand arose alongside my joy. I struggled with a sense of surprise, confusion, even shock. The sound of the Hebrew spoken by most of the people there was strange to me—I had studied Hebrew, but never actually tried to speak the language. The reception we received was something of a disappointment. Everyone seemed so casual. I had naively thought that all those present would come kiss us, rejoicing at our safe arrival in Israel. Yet no one paid any attention to us except the Jewish Agency people.

"*B'ruchim haba'im*," they said, and the welcome was translated for us. Officials began to register our names and to take down information about our families.

They told me that I had to be given a new name, a Hebrew name. That bothered me. "There is nothing wrong with my name," I protested. "It was a gift from my father. No one can give an Ethiopian child his name except his father or grandfather. Why change it?"

But the translators did not repeat this as I had said it. I spoke English, and came to an agreement with the officials that I would translate my name from the Amharic to its Hebrew equivalent. Yet I was not entirely comfortable with this arrangement. I would have preferred if in the record the Amharic name were also written.

For me, this was the beginning of culture shock. I felt as if I had come with something that was precious to me from my heritage, and had been told to dispense with it entirely in order to be absorbed into a new culture.

In the middle of the night we were all moved to different places. Yakov and I were to be taken south. An Ethiopian translator named Fasil provided his luxurious car for our transportation. As we drove, he briefed us about what to expect. "Being black is not a good thing in Israel, and it is certainly not the place for being an educated black," he said. "We are not wanted here."

Surely Fasil didn't intend to do so, but he threw me into confusion. I was already frustrated about the change in my name. What he now said was more than I was prepared to hear in my exhausted state. Hadn't our ancestors prayed for generations to be able to come to Jerusalem? My arrival was a special thing, the culmination of all those prayers. I wanted this to be a joyous moment, a time of fulfillment.

I had come with many expectations—to continue my education, to be materially comfortable—yet none was stronger than my desire to be free. The other things I hoped for required time and effort; but the freedom was mine because I was a Jew and I had arrived in the Jewish homeland.

All my life I had encountered difficulties because I was a Jew. In this land I had expected to be treated only as an equal; I had believed that all Jews would be my brothers and sisters. Until the translator spoke to me, it had never even occurred to me that I might be seen as less because of the color of my skin. The prospect that I would still be treated as different was unbearable.

I refused to simply accept what Fasil was saying. I noticed, for example, that even though he was complaining, he was driving an expensive car—something he certainly could not have had in Ethiopia, and I wondered if he had lost sight of this because he was still suffering from his own culture shock. But while I sat there it was impossible for me to know the truth, and I began to worry that my skin color would work against me as I started my new life.

It was very late when we finally arrived at the absorption center, but even at that hour workers were waiting to greet us and to give us something to eat. The welcome was wonderful for me, especially since I was feeling anxious about how we would be received. Some of the staff knew English, and although I was exhausted, I sat up to talk.

Yakov and I were given a small apartment to share. It was furnished with the basic necessities—two narrow beds, and a small table with two chairs. There was a private bathroom and a kitchen area, with a stove, a sink, and a refrigerator, and a couple of dishes and pots.

The next day, a Friday, we simply slept without knowing where we were. Someone woke us up and told us that we had to buy food for Shabbat. A small amount of Israeli currency had been given to us in the airport, and we were taken to a market and shown where we could get what we needed.

We bought a few things, returned, and went right back

to sleep. We were actually dizzy from exhaustion, since we had been awake for forty-eight hours straight during the course of our rescue. Now we were in no condition to prepare for Shabbat; we barely knew what was happening.

It all seemed strange to me. I remember saying to someone that first day, "Why am I here? This is not my place." The realization that we were expected to cook our own food hadn't dawned on us yet, since men never do such things for themselves in Ethiopia. Early on Shabbat morning, we found ourselves without food for the day, because we had bought chickens and other things, but hadn't given any thought to cooking them.

I have an older sister, Zehava, who was one of the lucky few who had been able to get into Israel directly from Ethiopia a few years earlier. At that time, she lived in Tiberias with her husband and their four children. Officials at the airport helped me to reach her by telephone, but I had not yet seen her. I made a request that we be allowed to go live in the absorption center near her, so that she could cook for us and help us. On Shabbat we ate only some cake that had been given to us at the airport. When we left for the new absorption center the following day, we carried the rest of the food we had bought with us.

The reunion with my sister was emotional; it had been years since we had seen each other. She kept laughing and crying at the same time. She stepped back for a moment to take a good look at me, and then leaned close to kiss me on one cheek and then the other, in the Ethiopian manner. She offered me food and fussed over me; she couldn't do enough for me.

I was the first other member of our family to join Zehava; although she had a family of her own, she had been painfully lonely for contact with other relatives. We drank one cup of coffee after another, reminiscing long into the night. It had been good for me to request the move; this family connection would be important for both of us.

Quite early the next morning, Zehava's husband, Malchi, took us to Jerusalem. A religious man, he was pleased to be the first to bring us to the Kotel, the Western Wall. From the moment we got on the bus to the Old City, I felt the excitement, and when the city walls came into view I caught my breath. This was the sacred place of our prayers, and it was in front of us.

It was a Monday morning, which meant Torah reading was taking place in front of the Kotel, and so it was very crowded. Yakov, Malchi, and I pushed our way through the crowd until we were up against the Wall itself. I ran my hands over the smooth stones, just to convince myself they were real. Then I closed my eyes in order to be alone with God in that place. I thought about all that had happened and felt an overwhelming sense of relief. I whispered a prayer of thanksgiving, as tears ran down my face.

Yakov and I then began to settle into the routine of the absorption process. We began Hebrew classes in the mornings, and soon learned how to handle such ordinary chores as cleaning our own room. I made it my habit to take my meals at my sister's home, and Yakov often accompanied me.

Our absorption center was a six-story apartment building, constantly buzzing with human activity—children running about, old people sitting quietly outside, young mothers with babies on their hips moving through the narrow hallways. Certain apartments were set aside as classrooms and office space. It was not unusual to see Israeli absorption workers going into one apartment or another.

Slowly, I began to grasp what was going on in my new environment, and what I saw distressed me. There was a great deal of misunderstanding at work in the absorption process. Among both the Ethiopians and the absorption workers were people of genuine good will—the Israelis were anxious to help the new immigrants integrate with Israeli society; the Ethiopians were eager to learn—but neither group really understood the other, so the interaction was not as fruitful as it should have been.

The Ethiopians studied Hebrew for a small part of the day; the rest of the time was spent doing nothing. The Israelis reasoned that since the Ethiopians had suffered in the refugee camps, they now deserved to rest. The Ethiopian point of view was quite different: they felt as if they had come to Israel to find "milk and honey" for themselves; now they were finding both, but without having to contribute much of their own effort.

Very few of the Israelis sincerely seemed to want to get to know the Ethiopians. Not many questions were asked about how we had lived in Ethiopia or about the culture we had left behind.

There is an expression used very often by Ethiopians, *Ishi*. This is usually translated as "Okay," but that does not really convey its meaning sufficiently. *Ishi* can mean at least half a dozen different things: "Are you joking?" or "I really will do it" or "Leave me alone" or "Don't worry, everything will be all right," etc. If the subtle meaning that is being conveyed is missed, then communication is lacking.

Body language also has cultural significance. Ways of using the eyes to express feeling, or shrugging the body, or waving the fingers can communicate a great deal.

The fact that the Israelis didn't understand our culture or our language, and didn't seem to want to learn, created problems for both of us. An obvious solution would have been to use the old timers—the Ethiopians who had been in Israel for some time already—not only as translators, but as mediators to bridge the gap. They could have served as transmitters of the culture, explaining what was happening to both the Israelis and the Ethiopians. But in order to do this properly they would have needed training, and they hadn't even been trained for their work as translators.

Ethiopians without much education, but with good native intelligence, were sometimes used for the work of translation, if they had learned their Hebrew well and seemed adjusted to Israeli society. A man who had been a farmer or who had been working on an assembly line in an Israeli factory might suddenly find he had a job translating for Ethiopian newcomers.

And yet his role was never properly explained to him, so he never truly understood what it could be. Most of the translators (there are exceptions) simply saw themselves as representatives of the absorption workers, and took it on themselves to tell us—the newcomers—what Israel was like and what could be expected. Unfortunately, a translator might not have understood Israeli life very well, and the information he conveyed may have been faulty. What is worse, if his own absorption had not been totally successful, he might have had hidden anger that he would inadvertently communicate to the new immigrants.

Some translators, anxious about their jobs, focused entirely on pleasing their Israeli employers. Since the Israelis, for their part, seemed primarily interested in getting the work done with as few complications as possible, the translators would communicate the words of the absorption workers to the immigrants, but were hesitant to translate the immigrants' statements back to the Israeli workers; they participated in what amounted to a one-sided process. "No, keep quiet," "No, don't go there," "No, don't ask for that," they would say, in order to avoid presenting their new bosses with difficulties.

The old timers who are translators, if properly trained,

could function quite well as social workers. They possess a first-hand knowledge of Ethiopian culture that an Israeli worker can never achieve. And yet, because the social workers are the ones with formal training, they are looked on as "experts"—and are eager to receive this credit—while the translators remain just translators.

One day I visited an Ethiopian family from Walkite. The man of the house, Yitzhak, had had a *gotah* in his house back in his village. If he earned some money, he would give it to his wife and she would hide it there. This was their secret place—they were the only ones in the world who knew what was in that *gotah*. Now, in Israel, when Yitzhak received a check, he would cash the entire amount and bring it home. He wouldn't think of putting it in the bank, because there it would be out of his control and he'd be forced to depend on strangers. Trust of that sort is something that has to develop slowly, through mutual effort.

In his new house, however, Yitzhak had a refrigerator. He didn't put his money in it, but that refrigerator seemed very much like the *gotah* for him and his wife: it was private, and food could be hidden away in there. While I was visiting, an Israeli absorption worker, a guide, entered the house. Without asking for permission, she went directly to the refrigerator and opened it to see how the family was managing to shop. "Why didn't you buy meat?" she asked. "Why did you buy this sour cream?"

Her intentions were good; her blunt manner was typically Israeli. But I saw the faces of Yitzhak and his wife. They were angry; their expressions had changed completely. No one would have invaded their privacy in this fashion back in Walkite. But the absorption worker, who was still talking, did not sense what was happening. She was not aware that she had angered the couple by violating their privacy.

Israelis openly express their anger; Ethiopians keep it inside. Someone sensitive to Ethiopian culture would have known how to read the change that had come over Yitzhak and his wife, but this woman was quite oblivious to it.

After she left, I asked the couple if they had understood her good intentions. "Was she in Ethiopia, helping us?" they asked. "Is it a new thing for us to raise children, to eat food, to wash ourselves and our clothes? It is enough if she tells us where to buy things and how to get what we need."

They felt that I, as an educated Ethiopian, should have protected them by telling the officials not to send such people anymore. But they did not realize that I could not interfere that way. "She is trying to help you to live a modern way of life, not hurt you," I said. "This will be over soon, be tolerant."

They did not understand how limited my own position was. When I had seen the absorption worker open their refrigerator, I had tried to explain to her what was happening, but she had ignored my efforts. Her attitude said, "An Ethiopian Jew is a 'primitive' and doesn't know anything." As far as she was concerned, she was the "expert," and since I was stereotyped as a "primitive," my human value was reduced.

The word "primitive" is used very loosely in connection with the Ethiopian people. The original anthropological definition was not meant to be derogatory. When people move from a simple to a more advanced technology there is always a cultural gap. But that gap can be filled easily without resorting to value judgments.

Technology is not the proper measure of human dignity. A man from a sophisticated society knows how to switch a light on and off, but if you ask him about the electrical circuit which powers that light, he may not understand how it works. This does not make him a "primitive" any more than a man from a rural village is primitive because he doesn't know how to switch on that light. An Ethiopian villager, dressed in his simple garments, may possess a world of human wisdom unknown in technological societies.

In the absorption process, a minority culture is absorbed by a dominant culture. The people from the minority culture suffer culture shock: they have to adjust to a new world—new ways of eating, new ways of traveling, new ways of preparing food. An Israeli caseworker trying to fit into Ethiopian culture would suffer the same kind of shock. It has nothing to do with superiority of one culture over the other.

Ethiopian society was traditionally oral. Here in Israel a serious mistake is made in thinking that an illiterate—one who can't read or write—doesn't know anything. A small child in the Ethiopian countryside knew how to do basic arithmetic very well; he might have used it for keeping track of his father's cows, for example. What he didn't know was how to write it down, using figures and signs for addition and subtraction. If you ask an Israeli child, who has been taught to do everything with pencil and paper, to manage these calculations in his head and remember what he is doing, he may be unable to oblige.

In Ethiopia, a father teaches his family on the evening of Passover; he doesn't read, he recites orally. And he understands what he is saying—he has no need of written material since he remembers it accurately without reading. In the West, these skills are less developed because they are not needed. But now Ethiopian Jews find themselves being judged by Israelis on the basis of a technology—the technology of writing and reading—rather than on their well-developed human capacities.

Most of our young people today are not illiterate, and those who do attend schools are excellent students because of the mental skills they have developed within the traditional culture. However, their problems multiply when they are taught to think of their old ways as useless. Because they aren't encouraged to value their unique heritage, they are quick to throw it away. Then, when they try to function as Israelis, they are suddenly confused and in trouble. Once our traditions are forgotten, it will be very hard to bring them back, and right now they are in danger of dying out.

It is a deeply ingrained fact of Ethiopian life that the man rules the family. Whether or not modern Western people agree with this is beside the point. Yet, when I was in the absorption center, wives were being taught that they were now their husbands' equals in financial matters. They were given joint bank accounts and encouraged to do the banking instead of their husbands. "You live in a democracy now," they were told. This was all very good and worthwhile, except that it created intense family quarrels.

Yakov and I felt we had to respond within the traditional norms of our society. We went to see three elderly Ethiopian gentlemen who were greatly respected, citing an Amharic expression, literally, "the grass of one's own country by its ox," meaning that something is done more effectively from within the culture.

"Why are you idle now?" I asked them. "In Ethiopia, you resolved critical situations between husband and wife. Your way is still useful. Use now it to minimize misunderstandings in the absorption center."

But the three elders were struggling with their own culture shock. "That worked in Ethiopia," they told us. Once they were convinced, however, they successfully used traditional arbitration to resolve family crises. And it was wonderful to see the change in them because they felt useful and in command of themselves again.

Youngsters in the absorption center, milling around

with too much time on their hands, were starting to get rowdy. After receiving their allotment of money, some of them were buying alcohol, and this was affecting their behavior. They would fight among themselves and with neighborhood Israelis. The situation reminded me of an English proverb: "An empty mind is the workshop of devils." The potential of these youngsters was being wasted. Their minds needed a focus, their energy a direction. It could have been provided by work or structured recreation. As it was, the young people had nothing to do with themselves and nowhere to go.

I went to the staff in the absorption center. "Please, find a way for these youngsters to produce something; help them to be busy. They must learn they cannot just continue to take all their lives. Let's teach them to give—it's very important."

I was crazy. I was bossy. I was simply trying to prove I knew better than they did, This is how most of the Israelis in the absorption center saw me.

A woman named Shira was one of the few people working in the absorption center who had tried to understand. She became my friend, and one night came to visit Yakov and me. Someone saw her go into our room.

On the same night that she visited, there had been a misunderstanding among some of the immigrants. In the morning, a meeting was called. On the side stood a housemother who would have liked it if I were gone. She was told that I'd had a visitor the night before.

After the meeting she called to me, "Shmuel!" Her tone was nasty. "I want you. I want you in my office." In my culture, you cannot summon someone with a finger, as she did me. It is as if you are calling a dog. But I went.

"Someone told me you were with a woman yesterday," she said to me.

"So what?" I wanted to know.

"She came to your apartment and was seen with you."

"What's wrong with it—if I did that? That's the whole purpose of being here," I said. "It's the best method of integration. It will invite marriage between us, and there will no longer be separate groups. That's why you are here—to help this happen. I want you to know that I did not do what you suspect. But you should encourage it. You are a worker of absorption, and you criticize me. Shame on you. Will you reject it if my son comes to your daughter tomorrow?"

"No! No!" she cried. "Shira is a worker of the Jewish Agency."

"So?" I said. "She's not my counsellor and not my teacher. To me, she is just a friend. We live in the free world, and she is a free person."

Three days after this, Shira lost her job. This was not a situation in which professional ethics applied. She truly was just my friend, and she was fired because she came to visit me.

We hadn't been in Israel long when absorption officials informed us that we would have to submit to a religious conversion process before our final identity papers would be issued. It didn't matter who actually brought the news to us—we understood very clearly that it came from the rabbinate.

In Ethiopia, we had suffered as Jews all of our lives. And we had believed that in Jerusalem we would be the same as all other Jews. Now it became clear that the rabbinate saw the matter differently. We were being told that we were only Jewish under certain conditions, and that our acceptance in Israel was based on these conditions.

Suddenly, I was seen as non-Jewish, and I felt inferior. Since it seemed I was just starting a Jewish life for the first time, it meant all the previous suffering I had endured in order to be a Jew was without value. At the same time, we had news of Ethiopian Jews dying in the refugee camps of Sudan, and it was almost too much for me—their suffering seemed so senseless.

What was required of me and the others was *tipat dam*—the ritual drawing of a drop of blood—and immersion in *mikvah*—*t'villah*. This had been the rule since Ethiopian Jews were first included under the Law of Return. The process was called *hidush*—"renewal."

In my absorption center there was a *kes*, always dressed in his traditional white robe, the *shamma*. He carried himself with enormous dignity; and when he prayed, he closed out the world around him. The tremendous frustration he was feeling showed in his eyes.

Most elderly people have more trouble adjusting to their new environment than young people do. This *kes* was no exception; he was struggling. But because he was seen as a leader, he was expected to show the others how to manage. He was painfully aware that people who had respected him in Ethiopia knew he was having trouble. But in addition, he had lost his religious status: the rabbinate had delegitimized him. All of the *keses* who have come to Israel have suffered this way.

Today, there is talk about the *keses* going to yeshivas for rabbinical training. They have the will, but their culture shock makes it very difficult, and at present few go. It will happen—Ethiopian religious men will graduate from rabbinic institutions. (There is one Ethiopian ordained rabbi now, but he had not been a *kes*.)

What is disturbing is that their status has become dependent on a culture that is not Ethiopian. It would have been far better if they had been accorded some status on the basis of what they already were, and then taught slowly over time. It could have been done with compassion.

At the beginning of 1985, the rabbinate ruled *tipat dam* no longer necessary for Ethiopian Jewish immigrants. This was a victory of great importance to us. And by July 1985, the rabbinate decided Ethiopian Jews no longer had to immerse in *mikvah* to be considered Jews. Now the question of Jewish legitimacy would be considered only at the time of marriage. This was another step, although not the final one.

Within Jewish law, all women are required to immerse in the *mikvah* before marriage. If an Ethiopian couple is told that the man must also immerse in order to confirm his Jewishness, there is a definite implication of conversion that is offensive to us. Our community is requesting that our own *keses* be permitted to rule on who is and who is not legitimately Jewish. Anyone who is a Jew should be treated fully as a Jew; anyone who is not ought to undergo conversion.

Rabbinic law (*halakha*) does provide a way for us to be legitimized, and we will prevail. But until the matter is resolved, patience is important. Volatile feelings can result in violence or suicides, or cause us to lose sight of the more urgent issue of Jews still waiting in Ethiopia. And if young Ethiopian couples refrain from marriage over the question of *mikvah*, our future will become shaky. We are not stronger than the rabbinate and may have no choice at the moment but to function within norms our society has laid out.

The absorption workers who brought us the news about our questionable status as Jews were themselves not truly observant Jews; for us this was incredibly ironic. In Ethiopia, we didn't have secular Jews, religious Jews, or orthodox, conservative, and reform Jews. Everyone was simply Jewish. In the villages, this meant that everyone went

to synagogue, observed Shabbat, read the Torah, and
prayed—all were Jews.

When we arrived in Israel, we found that some people
smoke and ride cars in Jerusalem on Shabbat. Our elders
were greatly angered. Our people are forbidden even to
walk long distances on Shabbat. "Where are we now?" our
elders asked. "It can't be Jerusalem."

The Ethiopians came wanting to live Jewish lives, and
ready to learn whatever is taught in Jerusalem. If there
was a gap between what they knew and rabbinic Judaism,
that was something beyond their control, which they were
willing to correct. Treated with respect, they would have accepted all of rabbinic *halakha*. But being told that we wer-
en't really Jewish destroyed our positive, eager attitude.

On several occasion over the last couple of years, young
Ethiopian Jews in Israel have taken their own lives. It is always young males who kill themselves, and most of the
time they do it by hanging. News of these deaths moves with
telegraphic speed through our community; the implications
are enormous and even those who did not know the victim
grieve. From across the country, Ethiopians travel to the
residence of the dead youngster to participate in the mourning; tears flow, women wail.

Our youngsters did not kill themselves in Ethiopia, or
even in the horror of the refugee camps. What they had was
hope—the expectation of their futures in Israel—and that
sustained them.

It's not hard to trace what happens when an Ethiopian youngster arrives and becomes ashamed of his old culture because of the confused absorption process. He feels
tense, overwhelmed by the new, more sophisticated culture.
A feeling of inferiority sets in—it seems that everyone else
knows more than he does.

He may be alone in the absorption center, without his

immediate family or anyone who knows him well. He doesn't speak about his stress; it's difficult for him to express his feelings because he's been taught to hold them in. Things happen that anger and upset him. Maybe he is called "Cushie," (a derogatory word for black in Hebrew) or "Falasha." He becomes depressed. And taking his life may seem like the solution.

There's an Israeli expression we hear frequently used: *Ba'yah shelcha*, "That's your problem." This concept is alien to communal Ethiopian culture. Within traditional Ethiopian culture relatives listen, care, and offer advice. Where no relative is available, a trusted elder within the community will do. What is most important is that Ethiopian youngsters in Israel today must know they are being heard. It would be wonderful if Israeli caseworkers understood and encouraged this process.

In Israel, Ethiopian Jews are sometimes asked, "Are you from Dimona?" Dimona is where the "Black Hebrews" from Chicago who have caused so much trouble live. Or we are asked, "Are you from America?" Israeli children are used to seeing black American sports figures on television. Within Israeli society, there is a basic lack of understanding of who Ethiopian Jews are and where we came from.

For a long time the media were silent about us because the whole issue of an Ethiopian *aliyah* was considered secret. That secret has been exposed. Yet because other Jews must be brought out of Ethiopia we are still being told it is a secret.

So many opportunities for increasing Israeli awareness of Ethiopian culture exist: television and radio could be used; newspaper articles could be written; and lectures provided in a variety of settings, with educated Ethiopians as well as trained anthropologists speaking. This could be particularly important within the school system. Every university in Israel should participate in educating the country at large about Ethiopian Jewish culture.

The Israeli absorption system is multibureaucratic. The Jewish Agency has a social service department, employing the translators and case workers, and an absorption department, employing the housemothers and helpers. In addition, there are government ministries of Absorption and Education. Every worker tries to be loyal to his own department, but varying rules and philosophies create competition in the field; the immigrants are the ones who suffer. We have a saying that applies here: "When two elephants fight, the grass is hurt."

A competitive system leads to an underutilization of certain professionals. Immigrants are often not sure of who is responsible for what. Each department, seeking credit for successes in the field, pulls at the newcomer: "See, it is because of what *we* did that things are good." The newcomers start to expect to receive, automatically, without giving. If the absorption were accomplished as a separate project with a single bureaucracy, many of these problems would be eliminated.

Ethiopian Jews are hardworking people. They understand the dignity of labor very well. No new immigrant should remain idle for more than the few weeks necessary to adjust and receive adequate rest and medical care. Everyone, including students not yet studying full-time, should be required to put in time each day in some constructive work that includes training. What is more, Ethiopians themselves ought to be participating in the planning of such work programs to give themselves the conviction of independence, and to prevent them from developing a passive reliance on an Israeli bureaucracy.

It is four years now since I have come to Israel. My absorption was painful, but successful. I am beginning to feel like a success in my work, although it was a tremendous struggle in the beginning. Demonstrating my skills, explaining myself, and defending my roles have all been hard.

But despite my struggles, I am not without hope. I love this land deeply. What is important is that it is mine, and I am a part of what happens here. And what is more, I expect our people to find their rightful place here. If they are given the opportunity, I know they will succeed. Their motivation is enormous; they have come to Israel surmounting great obstacles, and believing they will receive the education here that they greatly desire.

Even with the cultural bias and language problems that exist on intelligence tests, they score exceedingly well. Right now, over 370 Ethiopian students are studying at a post-high school level. The numbers will increase. I believe that it is the responsibility of everyone sincerely interested in assisting the Ethiopian Jewish people in Israel to help these young students. They must be encouraged in their learning, so that they can become self-reliant, productive citizens. And those who are educated must then be given an opportunity to serve their people as educators, community workers, and professional consultants for various programs designed to help the Ethiopian community.

Our problems can be solved, if they are approached with sympathy and good will. But, truly, they pale in significance compared with the suffering of those who still remain behind in Ethiopia. There is no higher priority than saving these lives. With the help of God, all of our brothers and sisters will come home. Whatever is required of us, it remains our task to keep alive the promise of tomorrow.

Ethiopian Jews In Israel

Women from Ashkelon gather at the Western Wall (Hakotel) on the occasion of the group Bar Mitzvah of their sons.

After his Bar Mitzvah this young man from Ashkelon poses proudly with his sister.

Young men from Ethiopia gather at the Western Wall for a group Bar Mitzvah.

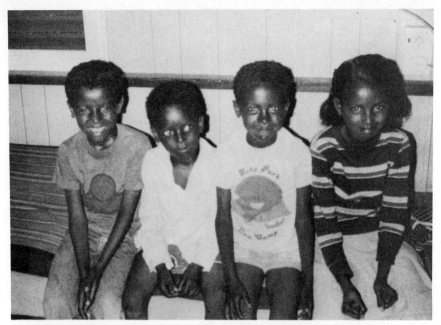

Three brothers and their sister pose in an absorption center in the north of Israel. (After the children and mother escaped, their father was arrested and tortured in Ethiopia.)

When the girl (left) was 3 months old, she was strapped to her mother's back for the death-defying walk to the Sudan. When they arrived, the child was so malnourished that there was little hope for her survival. Today, she and another 2-year-old play happily in an apartment in Beersheva.

Many Ethiopian Jews who arrive in Israel are placed in absorption centers. Here one family settles in, a few days after their long journey from the Sudan.

Ethiopian immigrants in traditional clothing gather on Mount Scopus for a Jerusalem Day celebration.

A proud Ethiopian immigrant poses with his son who was born in Israel.

Photographs
(1984-1986)

Ethiopian Jewish Life

An Ethiopian Jewish synagogue,1985. (© *Ilene Perlman*)

A *kes* (Jewish priest in English or *kohan* in Hebrew) blows the *shofar.* (© *Ilene Perlman*)

A *kes* takes part in a ritual slaughter, 1985. (© *Ilene Perlman*)

Holy men in Gondar City take part in Seg'd, 1985. (© *Ilene Perlman*)

A *Kes* holds a special Torah, 1985. (© *Ilene Perlman*)

A *kes* summons villagers to worship, 1985. (© *Ilene Perlman*)

This priest, or *kes*, contemplates a Hebrew prayer book, 1985. (© *Ilene Perlman*)

Men and women attend synagogue service, 1985. (© *Ilene Perlman*)

A *kes* recites the oral law, 1985. (© *Ilene Perlman*)

Three young villagers attend a religious service with their *kes*, 1985. (© *Ilene Perlman*)

Boys from several villages attend a Jewish school near Gondar City, 1985.
(© *Ilene Perlman*)

Ethiopian boy wears a *kipah* (yarmulka), 1985. (© *Ilene Perlman*)

Jewish woman holds her sleeping child in a *tukul,* a round house made of straw, 1985.
(© *Ilene Perlman*)

Menstruating woman confined to a special hut called a *mergem-gojo,* 1985. (© *Ilene Perlman*)

Ethiopian male proudly displays his Hebrew language book, 1985. (© *Ilene Perlman*)

Ethiopian Jewish Agency administrator arrives in a local village, 1985. (© *Ilene Perlman*)

Ethiopian woman displays clay figurines and pottery, 1985. (© *Ilene Perlman*)

Group of young males pose with their fathers, 1985. (© *Ilene Perlman*)

A recently-married young Jewish girl displays her imaginative carved sculptures, 1985. (© *Ilene Perlman*)

Woman with her child, 1985. (© *Ilene Perlman*)

A young man plays the *kirar,* a traditional string instrument, 1985. (© *Ilene Perlman*)

Elderly woman contemplates flight to Israel, 1985. (© *Ilene Perlman*)

Ethiopian Jews In Israel

Women from Ashkelon gather at the Western Wall (Hakotel), 1985. (© *Pearl Herman*)

Young men from Ethiopia attend a group Bar Mitzvah, 1985. (© *Pearl Herman*)

A young man from Ashkelon poses with his sister after a Bar-Mitzvah, 1985. (© *Pearl Herman*)

A family settles into their apartment in absorption center, 1985. (© *Pearl Herman*)

Young refugees gather in a Kiryat Arba apartment, 1985. (© *Pearl Herman*)

Two young girls play happily in an apartment in Beersheva, 1985. (© *Pearl Herman*)

Three brothers and their sister pose in an absorption center in the north of Israel, 1985. (© *Pearl Herman*)

Ethiopian immigrants gather on Mount Scopus for a Jerusalem Day celebration, 1985. (© *Pearl Herman*)

An Ethiopian immigrant poses with his Israeli-born son, 1985. (© *Pearl Herman*)